Diet recommendations during dialysis treatment

Please check these recommendations always with a nutrition consultant, therapist, doctor or dietician. The recipes and the list of ingredients are supporting the conventional medical therapy.
The calorie disclosures of fresh ingredients (fruit and vegetables) vary according to quality and time of harvest. The contents were checked by a dietician and a nutrition consultant for the Traditional Chinese Medicine (TCM).

Author:
©2019 Josef Miligui
www.ebns.at

AF206295

Source:
The lists are created from the EBNS database for nutritional counseling. The database is used by dietitians, therapists and doctors for advising the patient / client.

Literature:
The specialist literature and the training documents of the German and Austrian dietary and traditional Chinese medicine serve as a knowledge base. We have used the documents as a basis of knowledge, adapted it to our experience and completed them.
http://di-book.com

Production and publishing:
BoD – Books on Demand, Norderstedt
ISBN: 9783746097626

Diet recommendations for DIETETICS - Protein and electrolyte - kidney - dialysis treatment

1   Treatment strategy

Sufficient, high-quality protein supply, liquid supply according to the instructions of the treating physician, low in salt, low in phosphate, low in potassium.
Instead of salt use herbs and spices.
In order to counteract an increased protein degradation, the dialysis patient should also ensure adequate energy supply - the energy quotient should be 35 - 40 kcal per kg body weight.

The proportion of fats as energy source should be about 35 - 40 percent, the carbohydrate about 40 - 50 percent and the proteins about 15 - 20 percent.

Potassium reduction:
Fruits and vegetables from canned food contain half as much potassium as fresh fruit or vegetables.
Similarly, the potassium content of frozen food is much lower than fresh food.
By "watering". Potatoes or vegetables are cut into small pieces and watered in tenfold water over night, or the water is changed several times.
It should be boiled with a lot of water without the use of this water. By these measures the potassium content in vegetables can be reduced by up to 2/3.
The protein supply for dialysis patients should mainly contain biologically high-quality protein such as meat, fish, poultry, eggs, milk and dairy products.

2 Avoid

Potassium and phosphate rich beverages and foods, e.g. Salt, nuts, muesli, oatmeal, dried fruit, vegetable and fruit juices, bananas, apricots, not correspondingly prepared potatoes or vegetables, fresh or dried mushrooms and mushrooms. Potato products (mashed potatoes, potato dumplings), potato chips.
Processed cheese, salted cucumbers, smoked and cured meat and fish products such as raw ham, sausages, anchovies or salt herring, ready-to-serve meals, ready-to-eat soup, ready-to-eat sauces and ketchup.

3 Breakfast

	kkal. per serving
Baked chicory	230
Barley and vegetable soup	281
Barley mash with plums	106
Basic recipe for a chicken broth worming	89
Basic recipe for a vegetable soup, nutritious	47
Boiled celery salad with exotic spices	165
Carrot and potato rucola sandwich	94
Celery soup	101
Couscous Salad	338
Curdcheesedumplings on strawberry pulp	553
Fast polenta with avocado and spring onion	449

4   Snack

5   Lunch

6   Afternoon

7   Dinner

8 Any time

9 Recipes

(rec.) = You can use more.
(little) = You should use less than specified
(no) omit.

9.1 Asparagus and herb ragout

Diuretic, improves blood circulation, prevents cancer, dissolves stagnation, promotes weight loss. Good to fight immunodeficiency, loss of appetite, flatulence, high blood pressure, depressions, diabetes, diarrhea, stimulates liver function.
Cooking time approx. 30 min
Allergens: GL
4 portions to 465,5g. / 168kcal. - (carb:78% / prot:22%)
100g.=36,14kcal. / protein 7,54g. fat:4,09g.
µg. - Ph:2,55 Na:0,54 Ka:11,94 Mg:2,69 Ca:9,45 Fe:0,06 Zn:0,02 Col.:0 Hsr.:1,09

Quantity of ingredients:
Basic recipe for a vegetable soup (nutritious) 2 cups / 500g. (little)
Lemon peel 1/2 piece / 3g. (yes)
Coriander 1/4 teaspoon / 1g. (yes)
Nutmeg 1 pinch / 0,3g. (yes)
Asparagus (green or white) 1,8 lbs / 800g. (yes)
Parsley 1 Bunch / 125g. (yes)
Crème fraiche cheese 2 table spoons / 30g. (little)
Lemon juice 1 teaspoon / 3g. (yes)
Potato 7/8 lbs / 400g. (little)

Cooking instructions:
Cook potatoes with plenty of salted water about 20 min. until soft.
Heat the vegetable stock with lemon zest, coriander and nutmeg till it boil. Cook the peeled and sliced asparagus in it.
Drain asparagus in a sieve. Collect the cooking liquid.
In the blender mix 200 g of cooked asparagus (the lower ends), cooking liquid and parsley to a smooth sauce. Beat the sauce with crème fraîche until smooth. Add asparagus and heat again and season with lemon juice, salt and pepper. Serve with the potatoes.

9.2 Baked chicory

Mineral supporter and is full of A-B-C vitamins.
Cooking time approx. 20 min
Allergens: AG
2 portions to 460,5g. / 230kcal. - (carb:74% / prot:26%)
100g.=50,05kcal. / protein 6,05g. fat:7,04g.
µg. - Ph:10,03 Na:4,19 Ka:30,57 Mg:4,66 Ca:5,41 Fe:0,15 Zn:0,07 Col.:0 Hsr.:4,48

Quantity of ingredients:
Chicory 4 pieces / 500g. (yes)
Cream, sweet 30% 2 table spoons / 40g. (little)
Breadcrumbs (wheat bread, bread roll) 2 table spoons / 20g. (yes)
Rice Basmati 1/2 cup / 60g. (yes)
Water 3 cups / 300g. (little)
Salt 1 pinch / 1g. (little)

Cooking instructions:
Blanch chicory in hot water whole for about 5 minutes; place in a
casserole dish; put some sweet cream over it; put the bread crumbs
over the chicory and gratinate.

Place the rice in salted water, heat till it boils and let it simmer over low
heat for about 15 minutes.

9.3 Barley and vegetable soup

Supports urination, detoxifying, promotes spleen and liver, reduces
blood pressure, strengthens immune system, prevents cancer, reduces
radiation damage, promotes digestion, helps to digest fat, harmonizes
metabolism.
Cooking time approx. 2 hours
Allergens: AGL
3 portions to 304g. / 281kcal. - (carb:73% / prot:27%)
100g.=92,54kcal. / protein 11,93g. fat:5,74g.
µg. - Ph:9,75 Na:1,36 Ka:21,85 Mg:3,27 Ca:3,09 Fe:0,14 Zn:0,08 Col.:0,09 Hsr.:9,52

Quantity of ingredients:
Barley 1 cup / 120g. (yes)
Shiitake dried 1/8 oz / 4g. (yes)
Onion (shallot) 1 piece / 20g. (yes)
Cumin (Caraway seed) 1 knife tip / 0,5g. (yes)
Sunflower oil 1 table spoon / 10g. (little)
Water 1 cup / 250g. (little)
Celery sticks 2 branches / 20g. (yes)

Peas, green 5/8 lbs - 8oz / 250g. (yes)
Tomato 1 piece / 50g. (yes)
Carrot 2 pieces / 150g. (yes)
French beans Handful / 30g. (little)
Salt 1 pinch / 1g. (little)
Pepper (ground) 1 pinch / 0,5g. ()
Parsley 1 teaspoon / 3g. (yes)
Butter organic 1 teaspoon / 3g. (yes)

Cooking instructions:
Soak the barley in the evening for the next day. Soak the mushrooms separately at the next day. Brown onion and cumin in oil, then boil with water. Add the chopped vegetables, some salt, the barley and the shiitake mushrooms and cook everything to a thick soup. At the end, season with pepper, parsley and a little butter.

9.4   Barley mash with plums

Promotes spleen, diuretic, forcing spleen, supports urination, relaxes, reduces internal heat.
Cooking time approx. 25 min
Allergens: AG
5 portions to 289,6g. / 107kcal. - (carb:81% / prot:19%)
100g.=36,88kcal. / protein 3,15g. fat:1,57g.
µg. - Ph:1,2 Na:0,1 Ka:2,2 Mg:0,44 Ca:0,34 Fe:0,01 Zn:0,01 Col.:0,04 Hsr.:0,42

Quantity of ingredients:
Water 10 cups / 1200g. (little)
Barley 1 cup / 120g. (yes)
Plum 1 cup / 120g. (little)
Butter organic 2 teaspoons / 6g. (yes)
Sugar cane sugar 1/2 teaspoon / 2g. (yes)

Cooking instructions:
Grind coarse the barley and roast it dry. Add hot water, add ginger and cardamom and let it swell to a pulp in low heat. Core the plums and boil for 10 minutes with a little water. At the end, add the stewed plums, a little butter and sweetener.

Variant: If you want to go fast, you can use barley flakes instead of shot.

9.5   Basic recipe for a chicken broth worming

Strengthens blood, strengthens bone marrow, reduces blood pressure, strengthens immune system, prevents cancer, reduces radiation damage, promotes sweating, dissolves stagnation, good to fight loss of appetite, flatulence.
Cooking time approx. 2-3 hours
Allergens: L
9 portions to 244,89g. / 90kcal. - (carb:10% / prot:90%)
100g.=36,66kcal. / protein 15,68g. fat:11,56g.
µg. - Ph:0,86 Na:0,59 Ka:1,87 Mg:0,13 Ca:0,38 Fe:0,01 Zn:0 Col.:0,25 Hsr.:0,92

Quantity of ingredients:
Chicken meat 1/2 piece / 600g. (little)
Carrot 2 pieces / 150g. (yes)
Leek 1 stick / 45g. (yes)
Celery root 1 piece / 500g. (yes)
Ginger fresh 2 slices / 2g. (yes)
Juniper berry 1 teaspoon / 3g. (yes)
Bay leaf 3 pieces / 2g. (yes)
Water 4 cup / 900g. (little)

Cooking instructions:
Remove chicken parts from fat. Place chicken pieces in a saucepan with hot water and heat till it boils briefly, skimming any resulting foam. Add coarsely chopped vegetables and all spices and cook over medium heat for 2 to 3 hours. Strain the finished soup. Throw away vegetables and bones.
Tip: If you want to use the meat as a soup insert, take out after 45 minutes and return only the bones in the soup.
Refrigerate for later use.

9.6   Basic recipe for a fish broth

Strengthens the kidneys, promotes watering, reduces blood pressure, strengthens immune system, prevents cancer, reduces radiation damage. Low in cholesterol and protein rich. Improves blood circulation, stimulates appetite.
Cooking time approx. 40 min
Allergens: DLO
5 portions to 243,8g. / 128kcal. - (carb:34% / prot:66%)
100g.=52,34kcal. / protein 9,81g. fat:5,2g.
µg. - Ph:14,91 Na:7,09 Ka:31,5 Mg:2,39 Ca:4,63 Fe:0,11 Zn:0,02 Col.:0,01 Hsr.:11,94

Quantity of ingredients:
Fish pieces mixed (fresh water) 3/4 lbs / 300g. (little)
Celery root 1/4 lbs - 4oz / 120g. (yes)
Leek 2 inches / 10g. (yes)
Carrot 2 pieces / 150g. (yes)
White wine 1/2 cup / 125g. (little)
Lemon 1/2 piece / 50g. (yes)
Bay leaf 2 leaves / 2g. (yes)
Peppercorns 3 pieces / 2g. (yes)
Olive oil 1 table spoon / 10g. (yes)
Water 2 cup / 450g. (little)

Cooking instructions:
Fry celery, chopped carrots and leeks in olive oil, add bay leaf and
peppercorns, add pieces of fish and sauté briefly. Add water, add little
white wine or lemon. Simmer gently for 30 minutes. Skim off the
resulting foam several
times. In the end, sift the ingredients through a cloth.
Refrigerate for later use

9.7   Basic recipe for a vegetable soup, nutritious

Reduces blood pressure, strengthens immune system, prevents cancer,
forcing spleen, dissolves stagnation, promotes weight loss. Good to
fight immunodeficiency, high blood pressure, depressions, diabetes,
diarrhea, reduces blood lipids.
Cooking time approx. 2-3 hours
Allergens: L
5 portions to 240,6g. / 48kcal. - (carb:71% / prot:29%)
100g.=19,87kcal. / protein 1,56g. fat:1,31g.
µg. - Ph:0,97 Na:0,73 Ka:5,14 Mg:0,36 Ca:1,26 Fe:0,02 Zn:0,01 Col.:0 Hsr.:0,56

Quantity of ingredients:
Olive oil 1 table spoon / 4g. (yes)
Onion white 1 piece / 60g. (yes)
Carrot 3 pieces / 200g. (yes)
Parsnip 3/8 lbs - 6oz / 150g. (little)
Celery root 1 cup / 100g. (yes)
Ginger fresh 1/2 teaspoon / 2g. (yes)
Lemon 1/2 piece / 25g. (yes)

Juniper berry 6 pieces / 6g. (yes)
Thyme dried 1 pinch / 1g. (yes)
Lovage 1 table spoon / 3g. (yes)
Bay leaf 2 leaves / 1g. (yes)
Salt 1 pinch / 1g. (little)
Water 3 cups / 650g. (little)

Cooking instructions:
Cut the vegetables into cubes.
Heat oil in hot pot, fry shortly onions and vegetables.
Add cold water, then add ginger, bay leaf and lemon juice.
Season with juniper, thyme and lovage. Cover for 2 - 3 hours on a low heat and simmer.
The used vegetables should be thrown away.
The basic recipe serves as a soup base and to refine vegetables, legumes or cereals.
If you want to eat vegetable soup immediately, add the desired vegetables half an hour before.
Refrigerate for later use.

9.8   Basmati rice + Zucchini tofu dish

Diuretic, supports urination, harmonizes spleen and stomach, reduces flatulence, good to fight body overweight and high blood pressure.
Antioxidative, promotes digestion, perspiration, reduces blood lipids, forcing spleen.
Cooking time approx. 20 min
Allergens: E
4 portions to 306,75g. / 146kcal. - (carb:57% / prot:43%)
100g.=47,51kcal. / protein 7,95g. fat:4,89g.
µg. - Ph:13,21 Na:0,7 Ka:33,77 Mg:10,99 Ca:11,98 Fe:0,34 Zn:0,02 Col.:0 Hsr.:7,75

Quantity of ingredients:
Soy Tofu 5/8 lbs - 8oz / 250g. (yes)
Olive oil 2 table spoons / 6g. (yes)
Coriander 1/2 teaspoon / 4g. (yes)
Ginger fresh 1/2 teaspoon / 4g. (yes)
Rice Basmati 1/2 cup / 60g. (yes)
Water 3 cups / 200g. (little)
Zucchini 1 piece / 700g. (yes)

Cooking instructions:
Cut tofu cubes and marinate with olive oil, tamari, crushed coriander and ginger. Leave at least 1 hour.
Cook Basmati rice with the water. You can season with onion and cardamom.
Roast zucchini and tofu in pan in the hot oil for approx. 5-7 min.
Serve rice and tofu on a plate.
Add the parsley.
Can also be used as a salad for the home and on the go.

9.9   Beef pumpkin and vegetable stew

Reduces inflammation, improves digestion, reduces blood glucose, strengthens the muscles, tendons and bones, promotes digestion, helps to digest fat.
Cooking time approx. 1 hour
Allergens: AL
4 portions to 403,75g. / 369kcal. - (carb:48% / prot:52%)
100g.=91,46kcal. / protein 30,38g. fat:11,37g.
µg. - Ph:4,56 Na:3,23 Ka:16,05 Mg:1,7 Ca:3,71 Fe:0,08 Zn:0,08 Col.:1 Hsr.:2,83

Quantity of ingredients:
Beef meat 3/4 lbs / 350g. (little)
Pumpkin 3/4 lbs / 350g. (yes)
Leek 3/8 lbs - 6oz / 150g. (yes)
Potato 3/4 lbs / 350g. (little)
Tomato 3/8 lbs - 6oz / 150g. (yes)
Olive oil 2 table spoons / 25g. (yes)
Basic recipe for a vegetable soup (nutritious) 1/4 lbs - 4oz / 125g. (little)
Salt 1 pinch / 1g. (little)
Pepper (ground) 1 pinch / 0,5g. ()
Sugar cane sugar 1 pinch / 1g. (yes)
Parsley 1/2 bunch / 30g. (yes)
White bread (wheat bread) 4 slices / 80g. (yes)

Cooking instructions:
Dice beef. Peel pumpkin and dice. Cut the leek into rings and dice the peeled potatoes.
Brew the tomatoes with boiling water, peel off the skin and dice.
Steam the meat in olive oil and fill with vegetable stock. Add the cleaned vegetables. Season with salt, pepper, paprika, cumin and fructose.
Stew for 30 minutes over low heat.
Season again and sprinkle with parsley and serve with white bread.

9.10 Boiled celery salad with exotic spices

Forcing spleen, relieves diarrhea, antibacterial, blood-forming, blood detoxifying, reduces inflammation, diuretic,
improves blood circulation.
Cooking time approx. 30 min
Allergens: GLMNO
4 portions to 341g. / 166kcal. - (carb:48% / prot:52%)
100g.=48,61kcal. / protein 5,59g. fat:9,17g.
µg. - Ph:3,39 Na:6,17 Ka:17,47 Mg:0,76 Ca:5,05 Fe:0,03 Zn:0,01 Col.:0,2 Hsr.:3,02

Quantity of ingredients:
Celery root 1 1/2 piece / 900g. (yes)
Yogurt (natural, 3.5% fat) 1 cup / 250g. (yes)
Sour cream 15% fat 2 table spoons / 20g. (yes)
Turmeric (yellow root) 1 pinch / 1g. (yes)
Sesame oil 1 table spoon / 20g. (little)
Pepper (ground) 1 pinch / 0,5g. ()
Onion white 1/2 piece / 25g. (yes)
Black caraway 1 pinch / 1g. (yes)
Salt 1 pinch / 1g. (little)
Lemon juice 1 piece / 40g. (yes)
Apple (sour) 1/2 piece / 100g. (little)
Vinegar (Apple vinegar) 1 dash / 3g. (yes)

Cooking instructions:
Cook the peeled celeriac in thick slices and then cut into bite-sized strips.

Dressing: Mix a little yoghurt, sour cream, turmeric, sesame oil, pepper, lemongrass powder, finely chopped onion, a little mustard, salt, crushed black cumin, some cold water, lemon juice or vinegar; add the sour chopped apple, some rose paprika, the lukewarm celery and mix well; let it rest for 2 - 3 hours or overnight.

Ideal as a substitute for raw food

9.11 Broccoli cream soup

Strengthen your immune system, build and maintain healthy bones, teeth, hair and nails. Reduces blood pressure, strengthens immune system, prevents cancer, reduces radiation damage.
Cooking time approx. 30 min
Allergens: LO

6 portions to 251,17g. / 98kcal. - (carb:79% / prot:21%)
100g.=39,02kcal. / protein 4,17g. fat:1,91g.
µg. - Ph:1,14 Na:0,45 Ka:4,37 Mg:1,39 Ca:5,42 Fe:0,03 Zn:0,01 Col.:0 Hsr.:0,45

Quantity of ingredients:
Olive oil 2 table spoons / 7g. (yes)
Broccoli 1,1 lbs / 500g. (little)
Carrot 2 pieces / 150g. (yes)
Potato 2 pieces / 120g. (little)
Onion white 1 piece / 50g. (yes)
Water 1 cup / 50g. (little)
Basic recipe for a vegetable soup (nutritious) 2 cup / 500g. (little)
White wine 1/2 cup / 125g. (little)
Sage 1 teaspoon / 2g. (yes)
Rosemary 1 teaspoon / 2g. (yes)
Pepper (ground) 1 pinch / 0,5g. ()
Salt 1 pinch / 1g. (little)

Cooking instructions:
Add the olive oil to the pan, add the washed and cut broccoli, diced carrots and potatoes, sauté for a short time, add the chopped onion, fill with water, enough water to cover the vegetables at least 3 finger breadths. Add bouillon, salt, add a little bit of white wine, add the seasoned sage and rosemary.
Heat till it boils and then simmer on a small fire for about 25 minutes. Season with pepper, if necessary season with sea salt. Purée the soup.

9.12 Carrot and potato rucola sandwich

Reduces inflammation, improves digestion, supports urination, lowers cholesterol, strengthens immune system, prevents cancer, good to fight constipation (Fibre-rich), dissolves stagnation.
Cooking time approx. 20 min
Allergens: AG
4 portions to 116,25g. / 94kcal. - (carb:55% / prot:45%)
100g.=80,86kcal. / protein 2,68g. fat:2,83g.
µg. - Ph:4,15 Na:4,56 Ka:16,7 Mg:1,23 Ca:1,78 Fe:0,06 Zn:0,03 Col.:0,25 Hsr.:1,27

Quantity of ingredients:
Potato (mealy) 5/8 oz / 200g. (little)
Carrot 1 piece / 50g. (yes)
Sour cream 15% fat 3 table spoons / 45g. (yes)
Onion (spring onion) 1 piece / 20g. (yes)
Rucola 1/2 bunch / 100g. ()

Lemon peel 1/4 teaspoon / 1g. (yes)
Salt 1 pinch / 1g. (little)
Pepper (ground) 1 pinch / 0,2g. ()

Cooking instructions:
Cook the potatoes gently, peel and squeeze through the potato press.
Cook vegetable broth according to the basic recipe and remove a carrot after a short cooking time and finely crush with a fork.
Stir the potatoes, carrots, grated lemon zest and sour cream into a smooth cream.
Mix carrot and potato cream with finely chopped rocket salad. Season the spread with salt and pepper and spread the bread. Sprinkle with the finely chopped young onions.

9.13 Celery soup

Forcing spleen, calms nerves, stimulates appetite and digestion, dissolves stagnation.
Cooking time approx. 45 min
Allergens: ACGL
4 portions to 285,5g. / 101kcal. - (carb:44% / prot:56%)
100g.=35,38kcal. / protein 4,32g. fat:5,7g.
µg. - Ph:2,76 Na:5,05 Ka:11,06 Mg:0,62 Ca:2,85 Fe:0,03 Zn:0,01 Col.:1,44 Hsr.:2,12

Quantity of ingredients:
Water 2 cup / 500g. (little)
Butter organic 1 table spoon / 15g. (yes)
Nutmeg 1 pinch / 1g. (yes)
Salt 1 pinch / 1g. (little)
Spelled wholemeal flour 2-3 teaspoons / 25g. (little)
Celery root 1 piece / 500g. (yes)
Chicken egg 1 piece / 55g. (yes)
Cream sour 10% 2 table spoons / 25g. (yes)
Celery sticks 2 table spoons / 20g. (yes)
Pepper (ground) 1 pinch / 0,5g. ()

Cooking instructions:
In a hot saucepan, melt 1 tbsp butter; add a pinch of nutmeg, a pinch of salt, 1/2 cup wholegrain spelled flour (finely ground as fresh as possible) and stir to a sweat while stirring; add 1/2 liter of hot water gradually; add 1 large finely chopped celery tuber; cook for about 35 minutes and then puree; mix 1 egg yolk with 1 cup of cream; in the hot - no longer boiling! - soup vigorously; add some celery leaves finely chopped; with pepper, salt to taste.

9.14 Chicken soup with egg yolk and parsley

Strengthens blood, strengthens bone marrow, reduces blood pressure, strengthens immune system. Parsley stimulates liver function, harmonizes liver and spleen, strengthens eyesight, detoxifying.
Cooking time approx. 10 min
Allergens: CL
2 portions to 260g. / 118kcal. - (carb:82% / prot:18%)
100g.=45,19kcal. / protein 16,35g. fat:2,49g.
µg. - Ph:6,98 Na:8,83 Ka:9 Mg:24,79 Ca:69,4 Fe:0,28 Zn:0,05 Col.:6,52 Hsr.:2,22

Quantity of ingredients:
Basic recipe for a chicken soup (warming) 2 cup / 500g. (little)
Chicken yolk 1 piece / 10g. (yes)
Parsley 1 table spoon / 10g. (yes)

Cooking instructions:
Cook the chicken broth according to the basic recipe.
Heat broth and bubble the egg yolk. Sprinkle the chopped parsley over it and let it rest for about 2 minutes. Drink in small sips.

9.15 Cold cherry soup with curd cheese dumpling

Improves blood circulation, reduces inflammation, good to fight weakness, belching, diabetes, acute or chronic obstruction of the bowel. Laxative, stimulates digestion, cleans the intestinal flora.
Cooking time approx. 2 hours and more
Allergens: GO
2 portions to 307g. / 320kcal. - (carb:70% / prot:30%)
100g.=104,23kcal. / protein 7,97g. fat:15,18g.
µg. - Ph:12,34 Na:3,16 Ka:31,13 Mg:2,66 Ca:11,16 Fe:0,08 Zn:0,05
Col.:1,51 Hsr.:2,44

Quantity of ingredients:
Cherry compote 7/8 lbs / 450g. (little)
Agar agar (kelp) 1/2 teaspoon / 1,5g. (yes)
Curd cheese 20% 1/4 lbs - 4oz / 100g. (rec.)
Sour cream 15% fat 1/8 lbs - 2oz / 50g. (yes)
Vanilla sugar natural 1 package / 1g. (yes)
Sugar brown 1 table spoon / 10g. (yes)
Cinnamon ground 1 pinch / 0,5g. (yes)
Lemon peel 1 pinch / 1g. (yes)

Cooking instructions:
Strain the cherry compote.
Finely puree half of the cherries with the cherry juice using a blender and pass through a sieve.
Stir agar agar powder with cold water until smooth.
Bring the cherry puree to boil while stirring.
Mix in the agar-agar and cook the cherry puree for 1 minute while stirring.
Spread hot cherry puree on two soup plates.
Sprinkle the remaining cherries into the soup.
Cool down cherry soup for 2 hours until lightly gelled.
Use the hand mixer to stir the cord cheese, sour cream, sugar, vanilla sugar, cinnamon and lemon zest into a smooth, firm cream.
From the cream with the tablespoon, prick small dumplings and put them into the cherry soup.

9.16 Couscous Salad

Prevents cancer, forcing spleen, promotes digestion, stimulates liver function, reduces blood pressure, strengthens immune system, reduces radiation damage, diuretic.
Cooking time approx. 25 min
Allergens: A
3 portions to 285,67g. / 338kcal. - (carb:75% / prot:25%)
100y.=118,32kcal. / protein 12,21g. fat:7,11g.
µg. - Ph:5,1 Na:5,76 Ka:27,89 Mg:2,17 Ca:7,1 Fe:0,15 Zn:0,07 Col.:0 Hsr.:4,56

Quantity of ingredients:
Water 1 cup / 100g. (little)
Olive oil 1 table spoon / 15g. (yes)
Couscous 5/8 oz / 200g. (yes)
Lemon juice 3 table spoons / 30g. (yes)
Lemon peel 1 teaspoon / 2g. (yes)
Tomato 2 pieces / 80g. (yes)
Cucumber 1/4 lbs - 4oz / 100g. (yes)
Carrot 1/4 lbs - 4oz / 100g. (yes)
Parsley 1 Bunch / 100g. (yes)
Chives 1 Bunch / 100g. (yes)
Peppermint 3 twigs / 30g. (yes)

Cooking instructions:

Boil in a small saucepan 250 ml. water with salt and 1 tablespoon olive oil. Add the couscous, take the stove in the front and let it swell covered for 5 minutes. Put the couscous back on the stove and let it simmer for about 2 minutes with gentle stirring. If necessary, add 1 - 3 tbsp of hot water.
Mix the couscous with lemon juice, chopped lemon peel and 1 tbsp oil, season with salt and pepper and leave to set.
Add couscous with tomatoes, cucumber, parsley (all diced), carrots (grated), chives and mint (finely chopped). Season the couscous salad with lemon juice, salt and pepper.

9.17 Curdcheesedumplings on strawberry pulp

Strawberry forcing spleen and stomach, strengthens blood. Chicken egg calms nerves and stomach.
Cooking time approx. 30 min
Allergens: ACG
5 portions to 296,2g. / 553kcal. - (carb:40% / prot:60%)
100g.=186,77kcal. / protein 18,89g. fat:46,85g.
µg. - Ph:5,33 Na:3,67 Ka:5,89 Mg:0,95 Ca:2,43 Fe:0,04 Zn:0,02 Col.:2,41 Hsr.:0,72

Quantity of ingredients:
Curd cheese 20% 1,1 lbs / 500g. (rec.)
Spelled semolina 3/8 lbs - 6oz / 150g. (yes)
Butter organic 1/8 lbs - 2oz / 40g. (yes)
Chicken egg 2 pieces / 120g. (yes)
Sugar - icing sugar 2 table spoons / 20g. (yes)
Salt 1 pinch / 1g. (little)
Breadcrumbs (wheat bread, bread roll) 3 table spoons / 25g. (yes)
Butter organic 1/4 lbs - 4oz / 100g. (yes)
Strawberries 1,1 lbs / 500g. (yes)
Sugar - icing sugar 3 table spoons / 25g. (yes)

Cooking instructions:
Curd-cheese, grit, butter, eggs, powdered sugar and salt to a smooth dough. Keep the dough 15 mins in the refrigerator to settle down. Then shape small dumplings with a diameter of approx. 4cm and boil them for about 10 minutes in slightly boiling salt water. Heat butter in a pan and roast the breadcrumbs golden brown. Roll the dumplings carefully into the crumbs.
Serve the dumplings with the strawberry.

9.18 Duck with mung beans

Strengthens blood, forcing spleen, supports urination, promotes spleen and liver, reduces blood pressure, strengthens immune system, prevents cancer, reduces radiation damage, dissolves stagnation.
Cooking time approx. 2 hours
Allergens: E
5 portions to 354,2g. / 747kcal. - (carb:20% / prot:80%)
100g.=210,78kcal. / protein 56,76g. fat:46,01g.
µg. - Ph:8,02 Na:1,63 Ka:7,87 Mg:2,09 Ca:1,44 Fe:0,08 Zn:0,05 Col.:2,15 Hsr.:6,91

Quantity of ingredients:
Duck (slaughtered) 1/2 piece / 1250g. (little)
Onion white 2 pieces / 120g. (yes)
Carrot 1 piece / 120g. (yes)
Garlic 1 clove / 3g. (yes)
Mung bean 5/8 lbs - 8oz / 250g. (yes)
Peppercorns 3 pieces / 2g. (yes)
Honey 1 teaspoon / 3g. (yes)
Soy sauce 1 teaspoon / 3g. (little)
Lemon juice 1 teaspoon / 3g. (yes)
Salt 1 pinch / 1g. (little)
Pepper (ground) 1 pinch / 0,5g. ()
Olive oil 1 table spoon / 10g. (yes)
Bay leaf 2 leaves / 2g. (yes)
Black caraway 1 pinch / 1g. (yes)
Savory 1 teaspoon / 2g. (yes)

Cooking instructions:
The day before soak the mung beans and rinse the duck cold. Wash the vegetables, clean and cut into pieces. Put the duck and vegetables in a saucepan and cover with water. Add bay leaves, savory, mugwort and peppercorns. Boil over medium heat and simmer for 45 minutes. Skim off the foam. Remove duck from the stock, allow to cool and keep cool overnight.

In a saucepan, sauté the chopped onion in olive oil and pour in 1/4 liter of stock and add the pre-cooked vegetables. Add the mung beans and season with honey, soy sauce, lemon juice, salt, crushed black cumin and pepper.

Serve with rice or potatoes.

9.19 Fast polenta with avocado and spring onion

Good to fight inflammations, swelling, pain. Forcing spleen and stomach, lets urine and bile juice flow, dissolves stagnation. Includes unsaturated fatty acids, antioxidative.
Cooking time approx. 10 min
2 portions to 286g. / 450kcal. - (carb:55% / prot:45%)
100g.=157,17kcal. / protein 6,92g. fat:27,5g.
µg. - Ph:16,92 Na:0,99 Ka:54,42 Mg:8,7 Ca:3,02 Fe:0,13 Zn:0,17 Col.:0,01 Hsr.:3,78

Quantity of ingredients:
Corn (fast polenta) 1 cup / 120g. (yes)
Water 1 1/2 cups / 240g. (little)
Olive oil 1 table spoon / 15g. (yes)
Salt 1 pinch / 1g. (little)
Pepper (ground) 1 pinch / 0,5g. ()
Lemon juice 1 dash / 3g. (yes)
Onion (spring onion) 2 pieces / 40g. (yes)
Avocado 1/2 piece / 150g. (yes)
Turmeric (yellow root) 1 pinch / 1g. (yes)
Basil (fresh) 1 teaspoon / 2g. (yes)

Cooking instructions:
Heat water, add oil, lemon and spices.
When the water boils, add the polenta while stirring constantly and cook for 2 minutes.
When the porridge becomes firm, the polenta is ready.
Add diced avocado and sliced spring onion to the polenta. Sprinkle fresh basil on it.

9.20 Fish soup with rosemary

Promotes spleen and liver, reduces blood pressure, strengthens immune system, prevents cancer, reduces radiation damage, has little cholesterol and is protein rich, improves blood circulation, increases appetite. Antioxidant, forcing spleen, dissolves stagnation.
Cooking time approx. 30 min
Allergens: DLO
4 portions to 284,25g. / 271kcal. - (carb:38% / prot:62%)
100g.=95,43kcal. / protein 15,39g. fat:14,78g.
µg. - Ph:4,93 Na:1,8 Ka:11,89 Mg:0,76 Ca:1,33 Fe:0,03 Zn:0,03 Col.:0,01 Hsr.:3,59

Quantity of ingredients:
Basic recipe for a fish soup 2 cup / 500g. (little)
Rosemary 1/2 bunch / 7g. (yes)
Onion (spring onion) 1 piece / 20g. (yes)
Olive oil 2 table spoons / 35g. (yes)
Fish pieces mixed (fresh water) 5/8 lbs - 8oz / 250g. (little)
Carrot 1 piece / 120g. (yes)
Parsnip 1 piece / 180g. (little)
Celery root 1 slice / 20g. (yes)
Salt 1 pinch / 1g. (little)
Peppercorns 2 pieces / 1g. (yes)
Garlic 1 clove / 3g. (yes)

Cooking instructions:
Fry the onion and garlic in oil. Add fish broth. Add diced carrots, parsnips and celery. Season with salt and peppercorns. Simmer the soup on a low heat for 25 minutes.
Wash the fish, drizzle with lemon juice, divide into pieces and add to the soup with the pink rosemary. Cook for 5 min on low heat.
Add the chives and parsley and season the soup with the salt.

9.21 Halibut with tomato and garlic sauce

Promotes digestion, helps to digest fat, supports urination, reduces blood pressure, good to fight rheumatism, flatulence, bladder weakness, anemia, high blood pressure, depressions, diabetes, diarrhea. Valuable omega-3 fatty acids.
Cooking time approx. 45 min
Allergens: D
5 portions to 297,6g. / 319kcal. - (carb:36% / prot:64%)
100g.=107,19kcal. / protein 34,96g. fat:9,44g.
µg. - Ph:4,82 Na:8,78 Ka:7,08 Mg:1,03 Ca:0,88 Fe:0,02 Zn:0,01 Col.:0,82 Hsr.:4,78

Quantity of ingredients:
Rice variety any 1 cup / 120g. (yes)
Water 6 cups / 240g. (little)
Salt 1 pinch / 1g. (little)
Halibut (Flatfish) 2,2 lbs / 800g. (little)
Salt 1 pinch / 1g. (little)
Pepper (ground) 1 pinch / 0,5g. ()
Lemon juice 1 dash / 2g. (yes)
Bay leaf 2 pieces / 2g. (yes)
Lemon 1 piece / 30g. (yes)
Garlic 8 pieces / 10g. (yes)

Thyme dried 1 table spoon / 5g. (yes)
Olives 0,2 lbs / 75g. (yes)
Tomato 4 pieces / 200g. (yes)
Salt 1 pinch / 1g. (little)
Pepper (ground) 1 pinch / 0,5g. ()

Cooking instructions:
Cook rice with salted water (1:3).
Rinse the fish under running cold water, dab with kitchen paper and rub with salt, pepper and lemon juice.
Place the fish fillets in a casserole dish with pieces of bay leaf.

Wash the lemon hot and cut into slices, peel and halve the garlic.
Sprinkle the olives and the thyme over them.
Brew the tomatoes with hot water, skin and chop.

Mix all ingredients, season with salt and pepper and distribute around the fish.

Cook everything at 200°C/392°F for about 20 minutes.
Serve with the rice.

9.22 Lasagne with tofu cream

Harmonizes spleen and stomach, reduces Flatulence, protects the digestive system. Good to fight lack of appetite, flatulence, inflammatory bowel disease, stomach ulcers, rheumatism, heartburn, twelffinger intestinal ulcers.
Cooking time approx. 45 min
Allergens: ACEG
4 portions to 231g. / 301kcal. - (carb:50% / prot:50%)
100g.=130,3kcal. / protein 19,33g. fat:11,88g.
µg. - Ph:8,79 Na:3,51 Ka:7,05 Mg:4,06 Ca:7,27 Fe:0,09 Zn:0,05 Col.:3,83 Hsr.:3,82

Quantity of ingredients:
Soy Tofu 7/8 lbs / 400g. (yes)
Chicken egg 2 pieces / 100g. (yes)
Onion white 2 pieces / 120g. (yes)
Tomato 1/4 lbs - 4oz / 100g. (yes)
Oregano dried 1 pinch / 1g. (yes)
Marjoram 1 pinch / 1g. (yes)
Salt 1 pinch / 1g. (little)
Noodles (wheat, lasagne) with egg 3/8 lbs - 6oz / 150g. (rec.)
Edam cheese 1/8 lbs - 2oz / 50g. (little)

Cooking instructions:
Tofu cream: Mix tofu with eggs, onions, small tomatoes, oregano, marjoram, peppers and some sea salt put into a smooth mass using a kitchen machine with a knife or a blender.

Lasagne: Place 1/5 of the tofu cream in a casserole dish (25x15cm), cover with 3 lasagna leaves, repeat this process twice, and then finish the last fifth of the tofu cream over the pastry plates. Sprinkle with a little grated Edam and bake in the oven at 175°C/347°F for about 1/2 hour.

9.23 Leek and potato gratin

Reduces inflammation, improves digestion, regenerates skin, supports urination, lowers cholesterol, promotes sweating, dissolves stagnation.
Cooking time approx. 1 hour
Allergens: CGL
4 portions to 346,5g. / 368kcal. - (carb:56% / prot:44%)
100g.=106,35kcal. / protein 7,73g. fat:16,47g.
µg. - Ph:3,43 Na:5,61 Ka:14,59 Mg:1,08 Ca:3,84 Fe:0,04 Zn:0,03 Col.:1,24 Hsr.:1,42

Quantity of ingredients:
Potato 1,1 lbs / 500g. (little)
Leek 1,1 lbs / 500g. (yes)
Apple (sour) 1 piece / 200g. (little)
Crème fraiche cheese 1/4 lbs - 4oz / 125g. (little)
Basic recipe for a vegetable soup (nutritious) 1/4 cup / 20g. (little)
Chicken yolk 1 piece / 20g. (yes)
Emmental cheese 2 table spoons / 20g. (little)
Salt 1 pinch / 1g. (little)
Pepper (ground) 1 pinch / 0,5g. ()

Cooking instructions:
Wash the potatoes, peel, cut into very thin slices and pat dry. Place half in a flat greased baking dish.
Clean and wash leeks and cut into fine rings. Wash apple, peel and cut into thin slices. Spread the leek rings and apple slices on top. Put the remaining potato slices on top.
Mix crème fraîche, egg yolk, grated Emmentaler, salt and pepper, if necessary add some vegetable stock and pour over the casserole.
Bake at 200°C/392°F in the oven for about 45 to 50 minutes until golden brown. Cover with parchment paper after 30 minutes to prevent the burr from drying out.

9.24 Lentil and chestnut soup with curry

Reduces blood pressure, strengthens immune system, prevents cancer, reduces radiation damage, forcing spleen, dissolves stagnation, promotes weight loss. Good to fight immunodeficiency, loss of appetite, flatulence, high blood pressure, depressions, diabetes, diarrhea.
Cooking time approx. 45 min
Allergens: LO
4 portions to 238,25g. / 175kcal. - (carb:83% / prot:17%)
100g.=73,45kcal. / protein 4,17g. fat:4,33g.
µg. - Ph:2,67 Na:3,8 Ka:7,98 Mg:4,63 Ca:15,86 Fe:0,06 Zn:0,02 Col.:0 Hsr.:2,07

Quantity of ingredients:
Lentils red 3/8 lbs - 6oz / 150g. (yes)
Chestnuts 3/8 lbs - 6oz / 150g. (little)
Olive oil 1 table spoon / 10g. (yes)
Curry 2 teaspoons / 8g. (yes)
Basic recipe for a vegetable soup (nutritious) 2 cup / 500g. (little)
Turmeric (yellow root) 1 teaspoon / 2g. (yes)
White wine 1/2 cup / 125g. (little)
Anise (Common Fennel) 1 pinch / 1g. (yes)
Cardamom 1 pinch / 0,5g. (little)
Parsley 2 table spoons / 6g. (yes)

Cooking instructions:
Add the olive oil to a pan, sauté the chestnuts, sprinkle with the curry, add the lentils and season with vegetable stock, add a little white wine, mix in the curcuma, simmer for about 20 minutes (until the chestnuts are tender).
Then puree the soup.
Taste with a pinch of anise, cardamom and herbal salt. At the end, sprinkle finely chopped parsley over it.

9.25 Marinated cod on pumpkin puree

Reduces inflammation, improves digestion, promotes spleen, lung, stomach and kidneys, diuretic, reduces blood glucose, good to fight constipation and flatulence, dissolves stagnation.
Cooking time approx. 2 hours
Allergens: DG
4 portions to 288,5g. / 202kcal. - (carb:49% / prot:51%)
100g.=69,84kcal. / protein 17,24g. fat:5,13g.
µg. - Ph:5,4 Na:2,01 Ka:17,22 Mg:1,4 Ca:2,11 Fe:0,03 Zn:0,02 Col.:1,02 Hsr.:2,55

Quantity of ingredients:
Potato 6 pieces / 400g. (little)
Pumpkin 5/8 oz / 200g. (yes)
Onion white 1 piece / 50g. (yes)
Oregano dried 1/2 teaspoon / 1g. (yes)
Lemon juice 1/2 piece / 15g. (yes)
Salt 1 pinch / 1g. (little)
Pepper (ground) 1 pinch / 0,3g. ()
Crème fraiche cheese 2 table spoons / 30g. (little)
Yogurt (natural, 1.5% fat) 3/8 lbs - 6oz / 150g. (yes)
Oregano dried 1/4 teaspoon / 1g. (yes)
Basil (fresh) 1/2 teaspoon / 2g. (yes)
Cod 3/4 lbs / 300g. (little)
Salt 1 pinch / 1g. (little)
Pepper (ground) 1 pinch / 0,3g. ()
Olive oil 1 teaspoon / 3g. (yes)

Cooking instructions:
Mix yoghurt with oregano, basil and thyme. Wash the fish fillets, pat dry, place in a flat shape and pour over the marinade. Leave 2 hours in refrigerator.

Cook the potatoes in salted water until soft and peel.
Sauté the onion in oil until glassy, add the diced pumpkin and cook for about 10 min. Add oregano, lemon juice, salt, pepper and creme fraiche and puree with the blender.
Remove fish fillets from the marinade, drain, pat dry and salt. Coat a coated grill pan with 2 teaspoons of oil. Roast the fish fillets on both sides for 3 - 4 minutes and arrange with the potatoes on the pumpkin puree.

9.26 Noodle casserole with plugs and peaches

Relieves fatigue, relaxes, good to fight belching, acute or chronic obstruction of the bowel, flatulence, heartburn.
Calms nerves and stomach strengthens the defense, good to fight fungi infections.
Cooking time approx. 1 hour
Allergens: ACGO
4 portions to 293,5g. / 442kcal. - (carb:66% / prot:34%)
100g.=150,68kcal. / protein 17,55g. fat:19,06g.
µg. - Ph:6,51 Na:1,67 Ka:9,15 Mg:1,2 Ca:2,53 Fe:0,05 Zn:0,03 Col.:3,85 Hsr.:2,45

Quantity of ingredients:
Peaches 1,1 lbs / 500g. (little)
Noodles (wheat, ribbon noodles) with egg 5/8 oz / 200g. (rec.)
Chicken egg 2 pieces / 120g. (yes)
Sugar - icing sugar 1/8 lbs - 2oz / 40g. (yes)
Vanilla sugar natural 3 package / 3g. (yes)
Lemon peel 1/2 piece / 2g. (yes)
Cinnamon ground 1/4 teaspoon / 1g. (yes)
Curd cheese 20% 5/8 lbs - 8oz / 250g. (rec.)
Butter organic 2 teaspoons / 8g. (yes)
Strawberry jam 4 table spoons / 50g. (yes)

Cooking instructions:
Preheat oven to 180°C/356°F.
Put Peaches briefly in boiling water, drain and peel off the skin. Cut peaches into small slices.
Cook noodles in plenty of salted water until firm, drain, chill off cold and drain.
Separate eggs. Stir egg yolks with icing sugar, vanilla sugar, grated lemon zest and cinnamon until fluffy with the whisk. Stir in the curd cheese. Add the noodles.
Beat the egg whites into firm snow and carefully lift them under the pasta.
Spread a baking dish thinly with butter. Alternating pate noodle mixture and peach slices into the form layers. Finish with the pasta mixture.
Sprinkle the casserole with butter flakes and bake in a preheated oven for 3o minutes.
Serve portion by portion with a tablespoon of jam.

9.27 Noodles with turkeymeat and pineapple

Solves bile-, kidney- and bladder stones, provides Vitamin C, strengthens blood, strengthens bone marrow, reduces inflammation, supports urination.
Cooking time approx. 45 min
Allergens: ACGL
4 portions to 333g. / 292kcal. - (carb:53% / prot:47%)
100g.=87,61kcal. / protein 17,59g. fat:11,45g.
µg. - Ph:5,54 Na:3,01 Ka:12,71 Mg:1,78 Ca:4,2 Fe:0,05 Zn:0,05 Col.:0,98 Hsr.:3,07

Quantity of ingredients:
Noodles (whole grain) with egg 5/8 oz / 200g. (rec.)
Pineapple 5/8 oz / 200g. (little)
Water 1/2 cup / 50g. (little)
Turkey breast meat 5/8 oz / 200g. (little)
Rapeseed oil 1 table spoon / 12g. (yes)
Garlic 1 piece / 2g. (yes)
Basic recipe for a vegetable soup (nutritious) 1/2 cup / 100g. (little)
Cow's milk (whole milk 3.5% fat) 2/3 cup / 180g. (yes)
Fresh cheese 0,2 lbs / 75g. (little)
Curry 3 teaspoons / 6g. (yes)
Salt 1 pinch / 1g. (little)
Pepper (ground) 1 pinch / 0,5g. ()
Pomegranate 1 piece / 300g. (little)
Coconut flakes 1 table spoon / 6g. (little)

Cooking instructions:
Cook the noodles in salt water. Cut the pineapple into cubes and leave for 5 min. to simmer in water. Cut the meat sliced in strips and roast them in the oil. Add the chopped garlic and the pineapple sliced. Add about 50 ml of the pineapple juice and stir in the vegetable broth. Add the milk and the fresh cheese, then stir well until the fresh cheese is completely dissolved. Now add the curry and simmer for a few minutes until a creamy consistency is reached. Season with salt and pepper. Now add the noodles in the finished sauce. Cut the pomegranate and release the seeds. Distribute as many kernels on the dressed noodles. Whoever likes it can spread coconut chips over it.

9.28 Oat Congee

Strengthens immune system.
Cooking time approx. 2-4 hours
Allergens: A
3 portions to 275g. / 162kcal. - (carb:74% / prot:26%)
100g.=58,91kcal. / protein 7,04g. fat:2,87g.
µg. - Ph:5,76 Na:0,23 Ka:5,98 Mg:2,27 Ca:1,82 Fe:0,1 Zn:0,08 Col.:0 Hsr.:2,51

Quantity of ingredients:
Oat 1 cup / 125g. (yes)
Water 6 cups / 700g. (little)

Cooking instructions:
Cook oats and water in a ratio of about 1: 6. The amount of water determines the thickness of the mash (pure matter of taste). The oats swell, so do not take much. Put the oats in a saucepan with good insulation and a heavy lid. It is important to simmer the oats after a short boil on the slightest flame, otherwise it burns. Cook the oat for 2-4 hours. The longer it cooks, the more he strengthens.

9.29 Oriental rice pan

Forcing spleen, dissolves stagnation, promotes weight loss. Good to fight immunodeficiency, loss of appetite, flatulence, high blood pressure, helps to digest fat, strengthens kidney and bladder. Numerous vitamins, minerals and secondary plant active ingredients.
Cooking time approx. 30 min
Allergens: EL
6 portions to 271,83g. / 303kcal. - (carb:81% / prot:19%)
100g.=111,47kcal. / protein 9,51g. fat:5,44g.
µg. - Ph:2,35 Na:0,71 Ka:4,97 Mg:1,97 Ca:4,24 Fe:0,03 Zn:0,01 Col.:0 Hsr.:2,04

Quantity of ingredients:
Rice (whole grain) 3/8 lbs - 6oz / 180g. (yes)
Basic recipe for a vegetable soup (nutritious) 2 1/4 cups / 500g. (little)
Curry 1/2 teaspoon / 2g. (yes)
Onion (spring onion) 4 pieces / 80g. (yes)
Rapeseed oil 2 table spoons / 20g. (yes)
Peppers 1/4 lbs - 4oz / 120g. (yes)
Corn 3 oz / 80g. (yes)
Shiitake dried 1/2 oz / 80g. (yes)
Bamboo shoots 3 oz / 80g. (yes)
Peas 3 oz / 80g. (yes)
Peaches 1/8 lbs - 2oz / 60g. (little)
Pineapple 1/8 lbs - 2oz / 60g. (little)
Tomato 5/8 oz / 200g. (yes)
Lovage 1 teaspoon / 2g. (yes)
Basil (fresh) 1 teaspoon / 2g. (yes)
Parsley 1 teaspoon / 2g. (yes)
Lemon Balm (fresh) 1 teaspoon / 2g. (yes)
Pepper (ground) 1 pinch / 1g. ()

Cooking instructions:
Soak the mushrooms in water 20 min.
Boil the rice in the vegetable stock 15 min. and season with some curry.
Peel the onion, cut into fine cubes.
Heat the oil in a pan and sauté the onion cubes.
Wash the peppers in half, remove the core, cut into cubes and add.
Add corn, mushrooms and bamboo shoots, simmer 5 min. until firm.
Also add the bean sprouts, peas, peach cubes and pineapple cubes.
Then add the peeled, chopped tomatoes.
Add the cooked rice and season with the herbs and pepper.

9.30 Oven potatoes with celery-curd cheese (quark)

Promotes spleen, reduces Inflammation, improves digestion,
regenerates skin, supports urination, lowers cholesterol.
Cooking time approx. 30 min
Allergens: GL
2 portions to 398g. / 304kcal. - (carb:52% / prot:48%)
100g.=76,38kcal. / protein 15,61g. fat:24,04g.
µg. - Ph:19,06 Na:6,87 Ka:59,91 Mg:7,16 Ca:24,85 Fe:0,1 Zn:0,08 Col.:1,01 Hsr.:3,76

Quantity of ingredients:
Celery root 3 oz / 80g. (yes)
Basic recipe for a vegetable soup (nutritious) 1/2 cup / 100g. (little)
Lemon peel 1/2 teaspoon / 1g. (yes)
Salt 1 pinch / 1g. (little)
Pepper (ground) 1 pinch / 0,2g. ()
Lemon juice 1 teaspoon / 3g. (yes)
Curd cheese 20% 5/8 oz / 200g. (rec.)
Crème fraiche cheese 1/2 teaspoon / 5g. (little)
Potato 6 pieces / 400g. (little)
Olive oil 2 teaspoons / 5g. (yes)
Salt 1 pinch / 1g. (little)

Cooking instructions:
Celery-curd cheese:
Mix celery with vegetable broth according to basic recipe, caraway and
lemon peel. Cook for about 8 minutes until the celery is soft and the
vegetable broth almost evaporated. Mix the celery vegetable broth with
the lemon juice, finely, and stir until smooth. Season with salt and
pepper.

Baked potatoes:
Preheat oven to 200 °C / 400 °F.

Brush the potatoes well, halve them, and place them on a baking tray with the cut surface facing up. Lightly salt the surfaces and sprinkle with oil. Fry the potatoes in the oven for about 25 minutes.
Serve the celery plug to the potatoes.

9.31 Paprika-tomato rice

Good to fight little cholesterol, diabetes. Low in protein, low fat content, little protein. Forcing spleen, dissolves stagnation, promotes weight loss. Good to fight immunodeficiency, loss of appetite, flatulence, high blood pressure, depressions.
Cooking time approx. 25 min
Allergens: L
3 portions to 324g. / 291kcal. - (carb:89% / prot:11%)
100g.=89,92kcal. / protein 7,63g. fat:2,54g.
µg. - Ph:10,3 Na:1,31 Ka:15,5 Mg:9,5 Ca:22,5 Fe:0,14 Zn:0,06 Col.:0 Hsr.:4,12

Quantity of ingredients:
Onion white 1 piece / 50g. (yes)
Peppers 4 pieces / 120g. (yes)
Bay leaf 2 pieces / 1g. (yes)
Clove 2 pieces / 1g. (yes)
Basic recipe for a vegetable soup (nutritious) 7/8 lbs / 400g. (little)
Rice (whole grain) 5/8 oz / 200g. (yes)
Champignon 1/8 lbs - 2oz / 60g. ()
Parsley 1/2 oz / 20g. (yes)
Peppers (rose peppers) 1 pinch / 0,2g. (yes)
Tomato 1/4 lbs - 4oz / 120g. (yes)

Cooking instructions:
Finely chop the onion. Cut the peppers into fine strips.
Heat margarine in a saucepan, sauté onions and peppers, and rice. Add the vegetable stock, add cloves and bay leaves and leave to simmer in a closed pot for approx. 20 minutes. Cut the tomato meat into 1 cm cubes and add to the rice 5 minutes before the end of cooking.

9.32 Plum Cake

Cancer preventive effect, dehydrates the body, stimulates digestion and binds fats in the intestine, good to fight loss of appetite, flatulence, inflammatory bowel disease, obesity, gout, stomach ulcers, stomach cramps, rheumatism, heartburn. Relieves pain, detoxifying, bactericide.
Cooking time approx. 1 hour
Allergens: AG
6 portions to 307,83g. / 502kcal. - (carb:71% / prot:29%)
100g.=163,24kcal. / protein 12,32g. fat:19,28g.
µg. - Ph:2,65 Na:0,77 Ka:5,44 Mg:0,5 Ca:0,87 Fe:0,03 Zn:0,02 Col.:0,05 Hsr.:1,38

Quantity of ingredients:
Curd cheese 20% 5/8 oz / 200g. (rec.)
Wheat flour 7/8 lbs / 400g. (yes)
Cow's milk (whole milk 3.5% fat) 6 table spoons / 70g. (yes)
Rapeseed oil 6 table spoons / 70g. (yes)
Honey 8 table spoons / 100g. (yes)
Salt 1 pinch / 1g. (little)
Cinnamon ground 1 teaspoon / 3g. (yes)
Plums 2,2 lbs / 1000g. (little)

Cooking instructions:
Mix the flour, curd cheese, milk, oil, honey, salt and baking powder into a smooth dough. Keep the dough cool for 15 minutes to cool.
Lay out baking paper on a baking sheet and press the dough out to a bottom.
Now spread the plums evenly.
Sprinkle the cake with the cinnamon and bake for about 40 minutes at 190 ° C/374 °F.

9.33 Potato bags with wild herbs and tomato sauce

Promotes spleen, reduces inflammation, improves digestion, good to fight loss of appetite, flatulence, inflammatory bowel disease, stimulates liver function, promotes urination, dissolves stagnation, detoxifies, supporting prostate disorders.
Cooking time approx. 45 min
Allergens: ACG
5 portions to 346g. / 418kcal. - (carb:62% / prot:38%)
100g.=120,69kcal. / protein 16,87g. fat:16,1g.
µg. - Ph:4,46 Na:1,44 Ka:11,65 Mg:0,97 Ca:4,12 Fe:0,04 Zn:0,03 Col.:0,78 Hsr.:2,38

Quantity of ingredients:
Olive oil 1 table spoon / 10g. (yes)
Onion white 1 piece / 50g. (yes)
Garlic 1 piece / 2g. (yes)
Tomato puree 7/8 lbs / 400g. (yes)
Salt 1 pinch / 1g. (little)
Pepper (ground) 1 pinch / 0,5g. ()
Cream, sweet 30% 1 table spoon / 10g. (little)
Potato 1,4 lbs / 650g. (little)
Wheat flour 5/8 oz / 200g. (yes)
Chicken egg 1 piece / 60g. (yes)
Salt 1 pinch / 1g. (little)
Pepper (ground) 1 pinch / 0,5g. ()
Nutmeg 1 pinch / 0,2g. (yes)
Nettles 1/8 lbs - 2oz / 50g. (yes)
Dandelion (young plants) 1 oz / 30g. (yes)
Yarrow 1 oz / 30g. (yes)
Chervil dried 1/2 oz / 10g. (yes)
Parsley 1/8 lbs - 2oz / 50g. (yes)
Olive oil 1 table spoon / 10g. (yes)
Garlic 1 piece / 2g. (yes)
Curd cheese 20% 4 table spoons / 40g. (rec.)
Black caraway 1 pinch / 1g. (yes)
Pepper (ground) 1 pinch / 0,5g. ()
Emmental cheese 1/4 lbs / 100g. (little)

Cooking instructions:
Tomato sauce:
Heat oil. Roast diced onion briefly with crushed garlic. Add the tomato puree and let it thicken for 2 minutes while stirring, season with salt and pepper and add the cream and place in a fireproof mold.

Potato Batter:
Cook the boiled potato, drain, peel and squeeze. Mix in a bowl with flour, Parmesan, egg and spices. Roll out the dough on a lightly floured work surface and cut into 5 cm squares.
Herb Stuffing:
Chop the herbs and mix with oil, garlic, curd cheese, mayonnaise, herb salt, crushed black cumin and pepper to a creamy mass.
Put on the pastry with a spoon in the middle. Fold into a triangle, press on the edge and let the pockets soak in plenty of salted water until they float up. Add to the tomatoes, sprinkle with the grated cheese and bake in the oven until golden brown.

9.34 Potato gnocchi with vegetables and basil sauce

Strengthens immune system, promotes weight loss. Good to fight immunodeficiency, loss of appetite, flatulence, high blood pressure. Relaxing and reassuring.
Cooking time approx. 1 hour
Allergens: ACGL
4 portions to 290,25g. / 167kcal. - (carb:75% / prot:25%)
100g.=57,45kcal. / protein 6,54g. fat:4,63g.
µg. - Ph:3,26 Na:1,11 Ka:13,57 Mg:2,45 Ca:9,39 Fe:0,06 Zn:0,02 Col.:1,36 Hsr.:1,49

Quantity of ingredients:
Potato 5/8 lbs - 8oz / 250g. (little)
Wheat flour 1 oz / 25g. (yes)
Wheat semolina 1/2 oz / 15g. (yes)
Chicken yolk 1 piece / 20g. (yes)
Nutmeg 1 pinch / 0,2g. (yes)
Basic recipe for a vegetable soup (nutritious) 1 cup / 250g. (little)
Celery root 1/8 lbs - 2oz / 50g. (yes)
Lemon peel 1/2 teaspoon / 2g. (yes)
Ginger fresh 1/2 teaspoon / 2g. (yes)
Nutmeg 1 pinch / 0,2g. (yes)
Basil (fresh) 1 Bunch / 125g. (yes)
Crème fraiche cheese 1 table spoon / 20g. (little)
Salt 1 pinch / 1g. (little)
Pepper (ground) 1 pinch / 0,2g. ()
Carrot 1/4 lbs - 4oz / 100g. (yes)
Zucchini 1/4 lbs - 4oz / 100g. (yes)
Cauliflower 1/4 lbs - 4oz / 100g. (yes)
Broccoli 1/4 lbs - 4oz / 100g. (little)
Salt 1 pinch / 1g. (little)

Cooking instructions:
Steam the potatoes gently, peel and pass hot through the potato press. Process the hot potatoes with flour, semolina, egg, nutmeg and salt to a smooth dough. Let dough rest for 3o minutes.
Make small rolls (2 cm) out of the dough with flour-dusted hands, cut off 1 cm thin slices. To create the typical gnocchi shape, gently dab the dough pieces with your thumb. Leave the gnocchi in lightly boiling salted water for 6 - 8 minutes. Lift the gnocchi out of the pot with the skimmer.

Heat the vegetable stock till it boils. Add diced celery, grated lemon peel, finely chopped ginger and 1 pinch of nutmeg. Cover and simmer for about 10 minutes. Using the blender, puree the vegetable broth, celery, chopped basil and crème fraiche into a smooth sauce. Season with salt and nutmeg.

Cut carrots, zucchini, cauliflower and broccoli into small pieces and cook covered in a sieve over steam for 8 minutes until firm.
Heat the sauce again and add to the vegetables and arrange over the gnocchi.

9.35 Potato with dandelion salad

Promotes spleen, reduces inflammation, improves digestion, regenerates skin, supports urinating, lowers cholesterol, detoxifying, reduces inflammation, forcing spleen and digestive system, detoxifying, dissolves stagnation.
Cooking time approx. 25 min
2 portions to 203g. / 162kcal. - (carb:70% / prot:30%)
100g.=79,8kcal. / protein 4,28g. fat:5,59g.
µg. - Ph:26,58 Na:13,03 Ka:176,11 Mg:11,88 Ca:27,41 Fe:0,61 Zn:0,28 Col.:0,01
Hsr.:14,22

Quantity of ingredients:
Potato 5/8 lbs - 8oz / 250g. (little)
Onion white 1/2 piece / 20g. (yes)
Sunflower oil 1 table spoon / 10g. (little)
Dandelion (young plants) 1/4 lbs - 4oz / 125g. (yes)
Salt 1 pinch / 1g. (little)
Pepper white (ground) 1 pinch / 0,5g. (yes)

Cooking instructions:
Cook the potatoes in salted water and cut into thin slices. Finely chop the onion. Now season the potatoes with oil, salt and pepper and add the dandelion and mix.

9.36 Pumpkin slices with spicy rice

Strengthens lungs and spleen, diuretic, reduces blood glucose, protects liver, for the drainage of the body overweight and high blood pressure, harmonizes liver.
Cooking time approx. 45 min
Allergens: AG
4 portions to 260,5g. / 438kcal. - (carb:59% / prot:41%)
100g.=168,04kcal. / protein 4,2g. fat:27,77g.
µg. - Ph:4,8 Na:1,27 Ka:11,64 Mg:2,02 Ca:3,02 Fe:0,04 Zn:0,02 Col.:0,25 Hsr.:1,33

Quantity of ingredients:
Clarified butter 1/2 teaspoon / 5g. (yes)
Saffron 1 Sachet / 0,1g. (yes)
Turmeric (yellow root) 1 teaspoon / 2g. (yes)
Rice Basmati 1 cup / 120g. (yes)
Water 1 cup / 120g. (little)
Salt 1/2 teaspoon / 2g. (little)
Pumpkin 6-8 slices / 400g. (yes)
Barley flour 1 cup / 10g. (yes)
Breadcrumbs (wheat bread, bread roll) 1 cup / 10g. (yes)
Salt 1/2 teaspoon / 2g. (little)
Pepper (ground) 1 pinch / 1g. ()
Butter organic 1 table spoon / 10g. (yes)
Cream, sweet 30% 1 1/2 cup / 300g. (little)
Barley flour 2 table spoons / 20g. (yes)
Chives 3 table spoons / 20g. (yes)
Dill 3 table spoons / 20g. (yes)

Cooking instructions:
Melt the fat in a small saucepan, add saffron and turmeric, lightly roast
over medium heat for about 1-2 minutes to allow the aromas to develop
(note: the spices should never be burnt). Add the rice for about 2
minutes stir fry, add
the salt, stir briefly and add the water, stir and close the pot with a lid.
Cook at low to medium heat until the water is almost completely
absorbed, then remove from the heat and set aside with the lid still
closed and let it swell. Do not stir! When the water is completely
absorbed, the rice is ready!

Mix flour, bread crumbs, salt and pepper. Moisten the pumpkin slices
with water or mashed egg, turn the slices in the flour mixture and fry
gently in butter until golden brown and the pumpkin is soft. Melt the
butter in a small saucepan, brown the barley flour in it and remove from
heat, add the sour cream, season with salt, pepper, add the chopped
herbs and pour the sauce over the fried pumpkin slices. Serve with the
rice.

9.37 Rhubarb cake with sprinkles

Laxative, antipyretic. Protects the digestive system. Detoxifying, affects anorexia, good to fight flatulence, inflammatory bowel disease, brittle nails and hair. Relieves pain, detoxifying, against dry skin, acne, eczema.

Cooking time approx. 1 1/2 hours
Allergens: AG
8 portions to 239,5g. / 476kcal. - (carb:72% / prot:28%)
100g.=198,64kcal. / protein 12,39g. fat:15,41g.
µg. - Ph:1,84 Na:0,16 Ka:3,72 Mg:0,47 Ca:0,65 Fe:0,03 Zn:0,02 Col.:0,01 Hsr.:1,51

Quantity of ingredients:
Wheat flour 7/8 lbs / 400g. (yes)
Cow's milk (whole milk 3.5% fat) 1 cup / 200g. (yes)
Honey 2 teaspoons / 5g. (yes)
Sunflower oil 2 teaspoons / 5g. (little)
Lemon peel 1 piece / 3g. (yes)
Salt 1 pinch / 1g. (little)
Rhubarb 2,2 lbs / 800g. (little)
Margarine 1/4 lbs - 4oz / 120g. (yes)
Wheat flour 3/4 lbs / 300g. (yes)
Vanilla sugar natural 2 pinches / 1g. (yes)
Cinnamon ground 2 pinches / 1g. (yes)
Honey 5 table spoons / 50g. (yes)

Cooking instructions:
Mix flour, grated lemon peel and salt.
Heat milk gently and mix with yeast and honey.
Then add the flour mixture and the oil and knead vigorously. Cover the dough and let it rise in a warm place until it reaches twice the amount. (about 30 minutes)
For the sprinkles, mix flour with vanilla and cinnamon, then add honey and margarine and crumble to a crumbly mass. Keep the sprinkles dough cool.
Lay out a baking sheet with parchment paper.
Knead the dough for the bottom again, roll it out, place it on the baking sheet and let it rise for another 10 minutes.
Clean the rhubarb, wash it, halve lengthwise and cut into pieces of approx. 3 cm. Spread the pieces on the rolled out dough and crumble the sprinkles over the cake.
Place the cake in the preheated oven at 175 ° C and bake for about 40 minutes.

9.38 Rice with parsnips

Rich in vitamins, minerals potassium and zinc. Good to fight blood circulation disorders, thrombose, risk of embolism, high blood pressure, a headache, heart attack and stroke, yeast infections.
Cooking time approx. 45 min
3 portions to 261,33g. / 206kcal. - (carb:78% / prot:22%)
100g.=78,95kcal. / protein 5,16g. fat:4,52g.
µg. - Ph:6,72 Na:0,7 Ka:31,66 Mg:2,54 Ca:3,53 Fe:0,05 Zn:0,07 Col.:0 Hsr.:4,06

Quantity of ingredients:
Rice variety any 1 cup / 120g. (yes)
Water 1 1/2 cups / 200g. (little)
Salt 1 pinch / 1g. (little)
Parsnip 3-4 pieces / 450g. (little)
Olive oil 1 table spoon / 10g. (yes)
Sage 1 teaspoon / 3g. (yes)

Cooking instructions:
Peel the parsnips and cut into slices. Fry for a short time in oil. Add the rice and fry again for a short time. Add the water and cook it at least 30 min. Sprinkle with fresh chopped sage.

9.39 Roasted millet with plum compote

Supports urination, promotes spleen and kidney, strengthens the defense. Good to fight fungi infections.
Cooking time approx. 30 min
4 portions to 218,25g. / 139kcal. - (carb:85% / prot:15%)
100g.=63,8kcal. / protein 3,57g. fat:1,24g.
µg. - Ph:2,99 Na:0,1 Ka:4,37 Mg:1,68 Ca:0,78 Fe:0,09 Zn:0,03 Col.:0 Hsr.:0,93

Quantity of ingredients:
Millet 1 cup / 120g. (yes)
Water 1 1/2 cups / 250g. (little)
Plum 1 1/2 cups / 250g. (little)
Vanilla pod 1 pinch / 1g. (yes)
Water 5/8 lbs - 8oz / 250g. (little)
Cinnamon ground 1 pinch / 1g. (yes)
Acerola fruit nectar or powder 1/2 teaspoon / 1g. (little)

Cooking instructions:
Roast millet briefly, pour over water, heat till it boils and let stand for 20 min. to swell.

Cook plums with water, vanilla and cinnamon 10 min. then strain. Add acerola and add to the millet.

9.40 Spicy avocado cream with cottage cheese

Anti-inflammatory, good to fight swelling, pain and itching, forcing spleen and digestive system, detoxifying, bactericide.
Cooking time approx. 15 min
Allergens: G
4 portions to 271,25g. / 614kcal. - (carb:39% / prot:61%)
100g.=226,27kcal. / protein 11,04g. fat:40,92g.
µg. - Ph:7,44 Na:14,84 Ka:19,28 Mg:1,27 Ca:2,23 Fe:0,03 Zn:0,03 Col.:0,06 Hsr.:1,09

Quantity of ingredients:
Avocado 2 pieces / 600g. (yes)
Pepper (ground) 1 pinch / 0,5g. ()
Salt 1 pinch / 1g. (little)
Lemon juice 1/2 piece / 15g. (yes)
Olive oil 1 table spoon / 10g. (yes)
Chili (pod or ground) 1 pinch / 0,5g. (yes)
Cottage cheese 1 cup / 250g. (little)

Cooking instructions:
Peel, core and purée avocados; add plenty of ground pepper, salt, lemon juice, rose paprika, a few drops of oil, chili, fresh chopped herbs, a pinch of salt; cottage cheese (about the same amount as avocado cream), carefully submerge.

Goes well with: Potatoes and millet, with which the avocado cream in combination with vegetable dishes, legumes or lettuce leaves a delicious meal. It is also very good as an appetizer, as a souvenir at parties and as a morning meal in the summer together with a mild dish of lentils or Adzuki beans and grated radish.

9.41 Spicy Tofu Vegetable Pan

Forcing spleen, relieves constipation, detoxifying, reduces inflammation, improves blood circulation, promotes sweating, dissolves stagnation, reduces flatulence, reduces blood pressure, strengthens immune system, prevents cancer, reduces radiation damage.
Cooking time approx. 25 min
Allergens: EN
4 portions to 329,25g. / 241kcal. - (carb:67% / prot:33%)
100g.=73,27kcal. / protein 7,37g. fat:7,32g.
µg. - Ph:3,76 Na:4,32 Ka:9,86 Mg:2,38 Ca:3,32 Fe:0,08 Zn:0,02 Col.:0,01 Hsr.:1,82

Quantity of ingredients:
Sesame oil 2 table spoons / 20g. (little)
Carrot 2 pieces / 100g. (yes)
Fennel 1 piece / 250g. (yes)
Leek 1 piece / 200g. (yes)
Salt 1 pinch / 1g. (little)
Turmeric (yellow root) 1 pinch / 1g. (yes)
Lemon juice 1 dash / 1g. (yes)
Soy Tofu 1 package / 120g. (yes)
Pepper (ground) 1 pinch / 0,5g. ()
Soy sauce 1 dash / 3g. (little)
Rice (whole grain) 1 cup / 120g. (yes)
Water 6 cups / 500g. (little)
Salt 1 pinch / 1g. (little)

Cooking instructions:
Heat sesame oil in a hot wok or a hot pan; fry the chopped carrots, fennel and leek slices; salt, a dash of lemon juice, turmeric, tofu cubes roast for 1 - 2 minutes.
Add the pepper and cook covered for about 5 minutes; drizzle with soy sauce.
Place the rice in salted water, heat till it boils and let it simmer over low heat for about 15 minutes.

9.42 Spring salad

Blood-forming, blood detoxifying, diuretic, good to fight stomach discomfort, improves digestion, diarrhea, helps to digest fat, supports urination, reduces blood pressure, detoxifying, reduces inflammation, diuretic.
Cooking time approx. 10 min
Allergens: AEMNO

4 portions to 214,25g. / 180kcal. - (carb:64% / prot:36%)
100g.=84,13kcal. / protein 7,68g. fat:5,56g.
µg. - Ph:14,38 Na:19,94 Ka:78,76 Mg:7,01 Ca:20,61 Fe:0,72 Zn:0,03 Col.:0 Hsr.:7,87

Quantity of ingredients:
Sorrel 3/8 lbs - 6oz / 150g. (little)
Dandelion (young plants) 1/4 lbs - 4oz / 100g. (yes)
Mung bean sprouting 0,2 lbs / 75g. (yes)
Cress 1/4 lbs - 4oz / 100g. (yes)
Chives 1 Bunch / 50g. (yes)
Tomato 2 pieces / 100g. (yes)
Parsley 1 Bunch / 50g. (yes)
Soy sauce 1 dash / 3g. (little)
White bread (wheat bread) 6 slices / 120g. (yes)
Vinegar Aceto Balsamico / 8g. (yes)
Olive oil / 8g. (yes)

Cooking instructions:
Wash all salad´s, mix and prepare the sauce as follows:
Mix tahini with mustard and balsamic vinegar, tamari, olive oil, chives
and half of parsley. Pour the sauce over the salad and sprinkle the
remaining parsley just before serving.
Serve with the white bread.

9.43 Thick pea soup

Supports urination, detoxifying, dissolves stagnation, improves blood
circulation, strengthens liver and kidney, strengthens immune system.
Cooking time approx. 2-3 hours
Allergens: AN
3 portions to 255g. / 123kcal. - (carb:47% / prot:53%)
100g.=48,37kcal. / protein 4,36g. fat:7,3g.
µg. - Ph:3,44 Na:0,25 Ka:7,5 Mg:1,22 Ca:1,55 Fe:0,06 Zn:0,04 Col.:0 Hsr.:5,21

Quantity of ingredients:
Peas, green 3/8 lbs - 6oz / 150g. (yes)
Water 2 1/4 cups / 550g. (little)
Sesame oil 1 table spoon / 20g. (little)
Onion white 1/2 piece / 25g. (yes)
Ginger fresh 1/2 teaspoon / 1g. (yes)
Ground 1/2 teaspoon / 1g. (yes)
Oat meal 1 table spoon / 15g. (yes)
Salt 1 pinch / 1g. (little)
Parsley 1 stem / 2g. (yes)

Cooking instructions:
Soak dried peas before cooking. Sauté sesame oil, onion, a little oatmeal, ginger and cumin in a hot pot; add the peas and simmer for 2-3 hours; add salt at the end and purée with a blender; garnish with parsley.

9.44 Vanilla cream with berries

Weakness, chronic constipation of the intestine, weight loss, laxative, detoxifying, blood detoxifying. Strengthens the defense. Good to fight fungi infections.
Cooking time approx. 15 min
Allergens: G
4 portions to 272g. / 278kcal. - (carb:24% / prot:76%)
100g.=102,21kcal. / protein 13,82g. fat:31,13g.
µg. - Ph:5,99 Na:1,61 Ka:8,18 Mg:0,86 Ca:5,24 Fe:0,03 Zn:0,02 Col.:1,06 Hsr.:0,45

Quantity of ingredients:
Curd cheese 20% 7/8 lbs / 400g. (rec.)
Yogurt (natural, 1.5% fat) 3/8 lbs - 6oz / 150g. (yes)
Sugar brown 2 teaspoons / 8g. (yes)
Acerola fruit nectar or powder 1 teaspoon / 2g. (little)
Vanilla sugar natural 3 package / 3g. (yes)
Cream (30% fat) 1/4 lbs - 4oz / 125g. (yes)
Strawberries 1/4 lbs - 4oz / 100g. (yes)
Raspberry 1/4 lbs - 4oz / 100g. (little)
Blackberry´s 1/4 lbs - 4oz / 100g. (yes)
Blueberry 1/4 lbs - 4oz / 100g. (little)

Cooking instructions:
Mix the curd cheese, yoghurt, sugar, acerola and vanilla sugar with a hand mixer or whisk until smooth. Beat the whipped cream very stiff, mix it under the cream. Arrange vanilla cream in portions with the berries.

9.45 Wheat semolina with olives-herb-sauce and salad

Protects the digestive system. Detoxifying, affects anorexia, good to fight flatulence, inflammatory bowel disease, obesity, gout, stomach ulcers, stomach cramps, rheumatism, heartburn. Dissolves stagnation, relieves fatigue.
Cooking time approx. 15 min
Allergens: ACGL

3 portions to 291g. / 245kcal. - (carb:77% / prot:23%)
100g.=84,08kcal. / protein 7,65g. fat:9,46g.
µg. - Ph:4,44 Na:2,51 Ka:6,39 Mg:7,97 Ca:30,53 Fe:0,1 Zn:0,04 Col.:3,02 Hsr.:2,72

Quantity of ingredients:
Cream, sweet 30% 1/8 lbs - 2oz / 40g. (little)
Water 1/3 cup / 65g. (little)
Wheat semolina 1/4 lbs - 4oz / 100g. (yes)
Chicken egg 1 piece / 60g. (yes)
Pepper (ground) 1 pinch / 0,5g. ()
Lemon peel 1 pinch / 1g. (yes)
Onion white 1 piece / 60g. (yes)
Olive oil 1 teaspoon / 2g. (yes)
Chives 1 table spoon / 7g. (yes)
Basic recipe for a vegetable soup (nutritious) 2 cups / 500g. (little)
Lettuce 2 handful / 30g. (yes)
Olive oil 1 teaspoon / 3g. (yes)
Lemon juice 1 teaspoon / 3g. (yes)
Oregano fresh 1 teaspoon / 2g. (yes)

Cooking instructions:
Mix cream and water and heat till it boils. Stir in the wheat semolina and
cook to a thick porridge and remove from heat. Whisk the egg and stir
in, season with pepper and grated lemon zest. Form with 2 coffee
spoons, dumplings and leave to stir in the slightly boiling vegetable
stock until the dumplings float up.
Chop the onion and roast it in olive oil in a pan. Pour the semolina
dumplings into the pan and sprinkle with finely chopped chives.

Wash salad and cut into thin strips. Season with olive oil, lemon juice
and oregano.

9.46 Yellow lentil soup

Strengthens heart and kidney, diuretic, promotes spleen, calms the
stomach, promotes digestion, strengthens immune system, prevents
cancer, reduces radiation damage, stimulates liver function,
antioxidative.
Cooking time approx. 20 min
Allergens: A
7 portions to 324g. / 155kcal. - (carb:73% / prot:27%)
100g.=47,88kcal. / protein 7,59g. fat:1,91g.
µg. - Ph:0,84 Na:1,47 Ka:3,19 Mg:0,35 Ca:0,64 Fe:0,02 Zn:0,01 Col.:0 Hsr.:1,11

Quantity of ingredients:
Lentils yellow 1 lbs / 500g. (yes)
Carrot 2 pieces / 150g. (yes)
Kohlrabi 1 piece / 300g. (yes)
Onion white 1 piece / 50g. (yes)
Parsley 1/2 bunch / 100g. (yes)
Turmeric (yellow root) 1 pinch / 1g. (yes)
Cardamom 1 pinch / 1g. (little)
Salt 1 pinch / 1g. (little)
Olive oil 1 table spoon / 10g. (yes)
Water 4 cup / 1000g. (little)
Lemon juice 1/2 piece / 15g. (yes)
White bread (wheat bread) 7 slices / 140g. (yes)

Cooking instructions:
Wash lenses well in a colander. Heat oil in a pot. Add finely chopped onion, sliced carrots, diced kohlrabi and spices, sauté and salt. Add the lentils and cover with water and simmer for 20 minutes. Add water as needed and season with salt. Sprinkle with fresh parsley or fresh green cilantro and drizzle with lemon juice.
Here you can also use red lenses. (same cooking time).
Serve with white bread.

10 Effects of food

10.1 Use ingredients: recommendable

Curd cheese 20%
Mediterranean fish (cod, plaice, haddock, sea eel, mackerel)
Noodles (wheat) with egg
Noodles (wheat, lasagne) with egg

Noodles (wheat, ribbon noodles) with egg
Noodles (wheat, spaghetti) with egg
Noodles (whole grain) with egg
Salmon

10.2 Use ingredients: yes

Adzuki beans
Agar agar (kelp)
Amaranth
Amaranth Pops
Angelica root
Anise (Common Fennel)
Arrowroot
Asparagus (green or white)
Aubergine
Avocado
Baking powder
Balm
Bamboo shoots
Banchatee (green tea)
barberry
Barley
Barley flour
Barley grass powder
Barley grouts
Barley malt
Barley not peeled
Basil
Basil (fresh)
Batavia
Bay leaf
Bean oil
Beans (green, fresh)
Bearberry leaf
Bitter Herb liqueur
Bitter melon
Black beans
Black caraway
Blackberry leaves
Blackberry´s
Black-eyed peas
Blackthorn (Sloe)
Blue mallow tee
Borage
Borage oil
Boxhorn clover seeds
Bread roll

Bread with carob kernel flour
Breadcrumbs (wheat bread, bread roll)
Brie cheese
Broad beans (thick beans)
Brussels sprouts
Buckbean
Buckwheat
Buckwheat (roasted) Kasha
Bulgur (cereals)
Burdock root tea
Bush beans
Butter (half fat)
Butter beans white
Butter organic
Carob flour, St. john's bread
Carrot
Carrot (Early Carrot)
Carrot juice without sugar
Cauliflower
Celery root
Celery sticks
Cereal coffee
Chamomile
Chervil
Chervil dried
Chicken egg
Chicken egg white
Chicken yolk
Chickpeas
Chickweed
Chicory
Chili (pod or ground)
Chinese cabbage
Chives
Chlorella (fresh water)
Chrysanthemum blossom tea
Cinnamon ground
Cinnamon sticks
Clarified butter
Clove
Coconut grated

Coconut meat
Coconut milk
Cooking oil
Coriander
Coriander (fresh)
Corn
Corn (fast polenta)
Corn (roasted)
Corn flour
Corn germ oil
Corn Grease (Polenta)
Corn silk tea
Corn starch
Couscous
Cow's milk (1.5% fat)
Cow's milk (whole milk 3.5% fat)
Cranberries
Cream (30% fat)
Cream 10% coffee cream
Cream sour 10%
Cress
Crispbread
Cucumber
Cucumber (spicy cucumber)
Cumin (Caraway seed)
Curcuma
Curd cheese 40%
Curry
Curry paste red
Daisy
Dandelion (young plants)
Dandelion juice
Dandelionroots tea
Dashi
Dill
Dyer's broom herb
Elderberry blossom tee
Endive salad
Evening primrose oil
Fennel
Fennel seeds ground
Fennel tea
Fenugreek (Trigonella foenum-
graecum)
Feta cheese
Flower pollen
Fox nut, gorgon nut, makhana
Freshwater fish
Fructose (glucose)
Garlic
Gentian root
Ginger fresh
Ginger oil
Ginger powder

Ginseng root
Gourd
Grapes red
Grapes white
Grapeseed oil
Green tea
Ground
Ground caraway
Hawthorn
Herbal tea mix
Herbs bitter
Herbs of Provence
Herbs various
Herbs wild
Hibiscus
Hibiscus tea
Hokkaido pumpkin
Honey
Hop
Horehound leaves
Hyssop
Iceberg lettuce
Jasmine blossoms tee
Juniper berry
Kidney beans (red)
King Solomon's-seal
Kohlrabi
Kukicha tea
Lamb's lettuce
Lamb's lettuce
Lavender blossoms
Leaf salads (bitter)
Leek
Lemon
Lemon Balm (dried)
Lemon Balm (fresh)
Lemon juice
Lemon peel
Lemongrass
Lentils
Lentils black
Lentils red
Lentils yellow
Lettuce
Licorice root tea
Lima beans
Lime
Lime blossom tea
Liver smoothing tea
Longane
Lotus roots
Lotus seeds
Lovage
Lovage seeds

Mallow (Malva sylvestris) blossom tea
Malt
Maple syrup
Margarine
Margarine (diet)
Marjoram
Mayonnaise 50%
Mayonnaise 80%
Millet
Millet flakes
Mold cheese
Mulled Wine Spice
Multi-grain bread (gray bread)
Mung bean
Mung bean sprouting
Nasturtium (nose-twister or nose-tweaker)
Nettles
Nori, purple seaweed, red algae
Nutmeg
Oat
Oat flakes (whole grain)
Oat flakes roasted
Oat flour
Oat fusion (baby food)
Oat meal
Oat milk
Olive oil
Olives
Olives green
Onion (shallot)
Onion (spring onion)
Onion read
Onion white
Oregano dried
Oregano fresh
Palm oil
Parsley
Parsley root
Passion blossoms tea
Pearl barley
Pearl barley
Peas
Peas, green
Pepper Cayenne
Pepper powder (hot)
Pepper white (ground)
Peppercorns
Peppermint
Peppermint tea
Pepperoni
Pepperoni, red, pitted, halved
Pepperoni, yellow, pitted, halved
Peppers

Peppers (rose peppers)
Peppers (sweet)
Peppers powder
Pickle
Pinto beans speckled
Plaice
Psyllium seed
Pudding powder vanilla
Puff pastry
Pumpkin
Quinoa
Radicchio
Radish
Radish (white, green, purple-red)
Radish black
Radish horseradish
Radish leaves
Rapeseed oil
Raspberry leaf tea
Red berry (without sugar)
Ribworttea
Rice (fragrance)
Rice (Gaoliang / Sorghum)
Rice (whole grain)
Rice Basmati
Rice black
Rice flour
Rice long grain rice
Rice malt
Rice mash
Rice noodles
Rice red
Rice round grain
Rice starch
Rice sticky
Rice sweet
Rice variety any
Rice wild (nature rice)
Romaine lettuce / lettuce salad
Rose blossom tea
Rose leaf tea
Rosefish
Rosemary
Rusk
Rye
Rye flour
Safflower (Dyer's thistle / Hong Hua)
Saffron
Sage
Sago (cereals)
Salsify
Sauerkraut (cutted cabbage fermented)
Savory
Savoy cabbage / kale

Sea buckthorn
Sheep's milk
Sheep's milk yoghurt
Shiitake, dried
Sour cream 15% fat
Sour milk
Sourdough
Soy flour
Soy noodles
Soy Tofu
Soya Cuisine (soy cream)
Soybean milk
Soybean oil
Soybeans
Soybeans, black
Soybeans, blacks, fermented
Soybeans, yellow
Spelled flakes
Spelled grain
Spelled semolina
St. Benedict's thistle, blessed thistle, holy thistle, spotted thistle
Strawberries
Strawberry jam
Sugar - icing sugar
Sugar brown
Sugar candy white
Sugar cane sugar
Sugar fructose - fruit sugar
Sugar glucose - grapes sugar
Sugar Milk Sugar
Sugar molasses
Sugar palm sugar
Sugar substitute (sweetener)
Sugar white
Supplementary nutrition
Tarragon (Estragon)
Tea mixture uric acid lowering
Thistle oil
Thyme
Thyme dried
Tomato
Tomato puree
Tuna
Turmeric (yellow root)

Turnip
Turnips
Valerian
Vanilla
Vanilla pod
Vanilla powder
Vanilla sugar natural
Vinegar (Apple vinegar)
Vinegar (Red wine vinegar)
Vinegar Aceto Balsamico
Vinegar Aceto Balsamico white
Wakame
Water hot
Wax gourd
Wheat
Wheat bulgur
Wheat flakes
Wheat flatbread/pita bread
Wheat flour
Wheat semolina
Wheat semolina for children
Wheatgrass juice
Wheatgrass powder
White beans
White bread (baguette)
White bread (pretzel sticks)
White bread (roll)
White bread (wheat bread)
White breadcrumbs
White cabbage
White dumpling bread (wheat bread cut into chunks)
Whitefish
Wild garlic (garlic spinach)
Wild herbs
Wild strawberries
Wormwood herb
Yam root, yam root tuber
Yarrow
Yarrow tea
Yogi tea
Yogurt (natural, 1.5% fat)
Yogurt (natural, 3.5% fat)
Zucchini

10.3 Use ingredients: little

Acerola fruit nectar or powder
Agave nectar
Agrimony
Aloe juice
Anchovy / Sardine

Apple (sour)
Apple (sweet)
Apricot
Apricot jam
Artichoke

Basic recipe for a beef soup
Basic recipe for a beef soup (warming)
Basic recipe for a chicken soup
(warming)
Basic recipe for a duck soup
Basic recipe for a fish soup
Basic recipe for a rice soup (Congee)
Basic recipe for a vegetable soup
(nutritious)
Beef bone marrow
Beef fillet
Beef heart
Beef heart (calf)
Beef kidney
Beef liver
Beef lungs (calf)
Beef meat
Beef meat (calf)
Beef meatbones
Beef Oxtail pieces
Beef soup meat
Beef stomach
Berries of the season
Bitter Lemon
Bitter liqueur
Bitter orange peel
Black tea
Blackberry jam
Blueberry
Blueberry dried
Blueberry jam
Broccoli
Buckwheat whole grain
Buttermilk
Calamari
Camembert
Cantaloupe
Capers in olive oil
Carambola (Star fruit)
Cardamom
Carp
Caviar
Channa-Dal
Chenpi (chinese tangerine bowl)
Cherry
Cherry (sour)
Cherry compote
Chestnuts
Chicken Blood
Chicken heart
Chicken liver
Chicken meat
Chicken stomach
Chinese pearl barley

Clementine
Clementines
Cocoa
Coconut fat
Coconut flakes
Cod
Codfish
Coffee
Coix (seeds) YiYi Ren
Compote (fruits of the season)
Cottage cheese
Crab
Cranberry
Cranberry
Cranberry jam
Cranberry juice
Cream sour 20%
Cream sour 30%
Cream, sweet 30%
Creamer
Crème fraiche cheese
Crucian
Currant (black)
Currant (red)
Currant (white)
Currant jam (black)
Currant jam (red)
Currant juice (black)
Currants (black)
Currants (red)
Dates red
Deer meat
Deer meat
Deer's Bones
Deer's kidneys
Duck (heart)
Duck (slaughtered)
Ducks egg
Dulse (seaweed)
Edam cheese
Eel
Elderberries
Emmental cheese
Fernet Branca (herbal bitter liqueur)
Feta cheese
Fig
Fish innards
Fish pieces mixed (fresh water)
Fish remains
Fish sauce
Flounder
French beans
Fresh cheese
Fresh cheese from soya

Fresh cheese with herbs
Freshwater crab
Fruit tea
Gail plum
Galangal
Garam Masala powder
Gelatin white
Gelee Royal
Ginkgo fruit
Ginseng liqueur
Goat
Goat and sheep's blood
Goat and sheep's brain
Goat and sheep's liver
Goat and sheep's milk
Goat and sheep's stomach
Goat cheese
Goose
Goose blood
Goose egg
Goose fat
Goose parts
Gooseberry
Gorgonzola
Gouda cheese
Grape juice red
Grape juice white
Grapefruit (Pomelo)
Grapefruit dried peel
Grapefruit juice
Grass carp
Green spelt
Greengage
Guava
Halibut (Flatfish)
Herring
Hijiki
Honey wine (Met)
Horse meat
Jellyfish
Kaki plum
Kalmus
Kefir
Kiwi
Kombu seaweed (Saccharina japonica)
Kumquats
Ladyfingers
Lamb bones
Lamb kidneys
Lamb liver
Lamb meat
Lamb shoulder
Linseed oil
Lobster

Loquate / Japanese medlar
Luo Han Guo fruit
Lychee
Lychee in Preserved
Mackerel
Mango
Manioc flour
Mare's milk
Medlar
Mirabelle plum
Miso
Miso black (fermented)
Miso paste (soy bean paste)
Mixed Pickles
Morel (black, dried)
Morel, dried
Mozzarella
Muesli
Mulberry fruit
Mullet
Mussels
Mustard
Mustard Dijon
Mustard medium hot
Mustard seeds
Mustard sweet
Mutton
Mutton
Nectarine
Octopus
Octopus
Okra
Orange
Orange blossom
Orange dried peel
Orange grated peel
Orange jam
Orange peel
Oyster shell powder
Papaya
Parsnip
Passion fruit
Peaches
Peaches (canned)
Peanut butter
Peanut oil
Pear
Perch
Pheasant
Pig blood
Pigeon
Pigeon egg
Pimento
Pineapple

Pineapple juice without sugar
Plum
Plums
Pomegranate
Pork Bacon
Pork brain
Pork fat (lard)
Pork ham
Pork ham cooked
Pork ham smoked
Pork heart
Pork kidneys
Pork knuckle
Pork Lard
Pork liver
Pork lung
Pork marrow bones
Pork meat
Pork skin
Pork stomach
Pork/beef sausage (smoked)
Pork's intestine
Potato
Potato (mealy)
Potato flour
Prickly pear
Prosecco
Pumpernickel (dark bread)
Pumpkin seed oil
Quail
Quail egg
Quince
Rabbit
Rabbit (wild)
Rabbit liver
Rabbit meat
Raspberry
Raspberry jam
Red beet
Red cabbage
Rhubarb
Rose hip
Rose hip tea
Rum
Rye wholemeal bread
Sake
Salt
Salt (herbal)
Sea cucumber
Seacrab
Sesame oil

Sesame oil roasted
Shark
Sherry (whine)
Shrimp
Shrimps
Skim milk powder
Slug
Sorrel
Sour cherries
Sour milk cheese 20%
Soy sauce
Spelled (Dark) bread
Spelled wholemeal flour
Spiny lobsters
Spurdog (spiny dogfish, Schillerlocken)
Star anise
Stevia (candyleaf, sweetleaf)
Sunflower oil
Sweet potato
Tabasco
Tangerine
Toast bread (whole grain)
Tomato dried
Tomato juice
Tomato paste
Tonic Water
Trout
Trout (smoked)
Truffle
Tsampa (roasted barley flour)
Turkey breast meat
Turkey ham
Umeboshi paste
Umeboshi plums (Japanese apricots)
Walnut oil
Water
Watermelon
Wheat bran
Wheat flour whole grain
Wheat germ oil
Wheat/Rye/Gray-black bread with yeast
Whey
White wine
Whole grain bread
Wholemeal flour
Wild boar meat
Wormwood
Yeast
Yew nut
Yoghurt vanilla

10.4 Do not use contra-acting foods

Almond
Almond marzipan
Almond milk
Almond puree
Apple juice (natural cloudy)
Apple puree
Apricot dried
Apricot nectar
Apricots
Apricots juice
Banana
Banana (cooking banana)
Beer (alcohol-free)
Beer (alcohol-reduced)
Beer (Pils)
Beer (Top-fermented German dark beer)
Berry juice
Black fungus mushroom
Blackberry dried (unripe fruit)
Blueberry juice
Bocksdorn fruits (Fructus Lycii, Goji, goji berry Boletus mushroom
Brazil nuts
Brown ale
Campari
Cashews
Champignon
Chanterelle
Chard
Cherry juice
Chocolate
Chocolate (Diabetic)
Cola drink
Cola drink (low calorie)
Dates dried
Eel smoked
Fig dried
Fruit mix juice
Hazelnuts

Linseed
Linseed (crushed)
Lychee liqueur
Lye roll
Mango juice
Martini
Mineral water
Mu Erh Mushroom
Orange juice
Oyster mushroom
Oysters
Parmesan
Peanut (roasted)
Peanuts
Pear juice
Pine nuts
Pineapple (from a can)
Pistachios
Plum dried
Poppy
Pork sausage (Bratwurst) Processed cheese 12%
processed cheese 30%
Pumpkin seeds
Raisins
Raspberry dried (immature)
Red wine
Reishi mushroom
Sesame paste (Tahini)
Sesame, black
Sesame, white
Soy Tofu smoked
Spinach
Spirit
Strawberry Juice
Sunflower seeds
Vegetable juice
Walnuts
Walnuts roasted
Wheat beer

11 Complementary

11.1 Bath for purification

preparation: Healing bath
A bath for purification (base bath), stimulates the natural regeneration of the skin and thus supports the excretion of acids and metabolic waste.
The longer you bathe, the more effective the bath is.
Purification bath additive available at the pharmacy or drugstore.

11.2 Horseradish

Armoracia rusticana
preparation: Different effects
Good against allergies, sinus infections, kidneys - u. Bladder infection,
bronchitis, rheumatism, head - u. Toothache.
Active ingredients: mustard oil split off glycosides, gluconasturtiin,
sinigrin, vitamin C, potassium
Too much can cause irritation in the stomach and intestines. Kidney lead.

12 Basics of Nutrition

The basic principles of nutrition described herein are general recommendations. They are not aimed at a specific form of therapy. Recommendations concerning a therapy have priority.

12.1 Nutrition

Regular meals in a relaxed atmosphere. A warm breakfast is considered a good start into the day.
The main meals ought to be taken for lunch – supper in the early evening. Pay attention to feeling hungry or sated: don't eat too much nor remain hungry is the rule
Prepare the meals freshly from natural, regional products. Frozen, heat-conserved, industrially prepared or foodstuffs cooked in the microwave oven are rejected.
Choice of foodstuffs according to the season: more cooling food in summer, more warming food in winter.
Eat cooked food at least twice a day. Food and drinks ought to be lukewarm, never ice-cold or hot.
Raw vegetables, briefly cooked vegetables, freshly squeezed juices and mineral water are not recommended. Milk and dairy products are only included in the diet if they don't cause problems.
Don't use therapeutic recipes over a longer period without consulting your doctor or therapist.

Varied food
Enjoy the diversity of foodstuffs. Characteristics of a balanced nutrition are variety, suitable combination and a balanced quantity of rich and low energy foodstuffs (on one hand avoiding undersupply with essential nutrients and on the other hand to take to many undesirable substances).

A lot of Cereal Products - and Potatoes
Bread, pasta, rice, cereal flakes (best wholemeal) as well as potatoes contain almost no fat, but many vitamins, mineral nutrients, trace elements, roughage and secondary plant substances. These foodstuffs ought to be taken with low-fat side dishes.

Vegetables and Fruit – „Take Five" every day ...
5 portions of vegetables and fruit a day, as fresh as possible, briefly cooked, or maybe one portion as a juice – ideal as a side dish to every meal as well as snack between meals: Thus a lot of vitamins, mineral nutrients as well as roughage and secondary plant substances

Daily milk and dairy products
Milk and Dairy Products every Day, once or twice per Week Fish; meat, sausages as well as eggs moderately. These foodstuffs contain valuable nutrients like calcium in the milk, iodine selenium and omega-3 fat acids in saltwater fish. Meat is favorable due to its high content of disposable iron and the vitamins B1, B6 and B12. Quantities of 300 – 600 g meat and sausage per week are sufficient. Prefer low-fat products, especially in meat- and dairy products.

Low-fat and fatty Foodstuffs
Fat supplies us with essential fat acids and fatty foodstuffs contain also fat-soluble vitamins. Fat is high in energy; therefore much fat in the food may cause overweight, possibly also cancer. Too many saturated fat acids may further a tendency for cardio-vascular diseases in the long term. Prefer vegetable oils and fats (e.g. rapeseed-, olive-, soya-oils and solid fats produced therefrom). Beware of invisible fat in meat- and dairy products, pastry and sweets as well as in fast-food and convenience foods. 70 – 90 g fat per day is sufficient.

Moderately Sugar and Salt
Take sugar and foods/drinks containing various kinds of sugar (e.g. glucose syrup) only occasionally. Use herbs and spices as well as a little salt creatively. Prefer salt containing iodine.

Plenty of Liquids
Water is absolutely essential. Drink 1-2 l liquids every day. Prefer water (with or without gas) and other low-calorie drinks. Alcoholic drinks should not be taken.

Tasty Dishes, carefully cooked
Cook the meals with as low temperatures and as short as possible, using little water and fat – this preserves the original taste, keeps the nutrients intact and prevents the production of harmful compounds.

Take time and enjoy the food
Take your Time and enjoy your Food
Eating consciously helps to eat right. The eye enjoys food, too. It's fun, invites to enjoy varied dishes and stimulates the feeling of satiety.

Watch your Weight and stay in Motion
A balanced diet and a lot of exercise and sport (30 – 60 min/day) are a healthy combination. The right weight furthers well-being and health. Thermals, directional effectiveness, digestive power

There are various criteria for judging the effectiveness of herbs and foodstuffs.
The use of certain herbs and ingredients is based on observations of the effects on the body which these foodstuffs, herbs and spices show after having eaten them. The medical science has developed following system: Every ingredient or herb has a directional effectiveness. Furthermore, there are herbs which have a special effect on certain organs.
The basic condition for a healthy metabolism is to obtain sufficient energy from food and that the digestive process doesn't use too much energy. An easily digestible meal makes content and sated, doesn't cause flatulence and fatigue after the meal. The perfect spices increase the healthiness of our meals. Very often, just small doses of herbs and spices will suffice. They are not used to make us sated, but to help our digestive organs to digest the food.

12.2 Recipes

The recipes list the ingredients to be used and the cooking instructions show how the dish is prepared. The list of ingredients shows the concerned quantities as well as the relevance for the therapy. If you find „less than mentioned", try to comply or find an alternative from the „list of recommended foodstuffs". Mostly it shall result just in a small change of taste when you simply avoid this ingredient.
Mild cooking methods: boiling, stewing, poaching, steaming
Strong cooking methods: barbecuing, roasting, frying, smoking
Balanced cooking methods: deep-frying, baking brick
Deep-freezing and warming in the microwave oven should be avoided (denaturalization).

12.3 Foodstuffs

Foodstuffs have an effect on body and soul like medicinal herbs, only a very much milder one. Dietary advice is mainly based on regional foodstuffs. The knowledge about the effects of each foodstuff and the knowledge, when which foodstuff shall be used, is based on the orthodoschool of medicine. Use ecologic-organic products, if possible. As everything should be cooked for a long time due to a better digestability and very rarely eaten raw, the food agrees with everyone.
The classification of the foodstuffs according to their effect on the body is the basis in order to achieve a harmonious status of health.

Dietary advisors do not recommend certain foodstuffs for everyone. The individual diet is tailor-made for the individual constitution.

Buy only fresh and ripe fruit and vegetables. You ought to leave unripe fruit and vegetables and such with brown spots and wilted leaves behind in the market. In this case take deep-frozen goods (never ready-to-serve dishes!). Fruit and vegetables are deep-frozen immediately after harvesting and often contain more vitamins and minerals than the goods from the vegetable shelf. Whereas conserved or tinned goods contain very much less biological substances. Also, salt, sugar and others are mostly added to the latter. Never leave the foodstuffs in the water after washing them to avoid that many vital substances get drowned. Clean salads, fruit and vegetables immediately before serving.

Please make sure of the hygienic processing of foodstuffs. Clean your salads, fruit and vegetables carefully. When cooking with meat, prepare all ingredients first and then process the meat products. Clean the worktop and tools very carefully. Wooden surfaces ought to be treated with a mild disinfectant regularly in order to reduce germination.

Store fruit and vegetables separately, if possible. Harvested fruit and vegetables are still alive and emit e.g. ethylene gas, which makes other products ripen and age faster. Keep meat and fish in the closed packaging or store them in the fridge in closed containers.

12.4 Herbs

There are some basic rules for storing medicinal herbs. On principle, herbs must be protected from direct sunlight, humidity and heat.

Containers for the storage of herbs may be glasses, ceramic jars and even plastic containers. However, plastic is a rather unsuitable material and should only be a short-term solution. In case of glass containers, use a dark material.

Medicinal herbs cannot be kept for any long period. The shelf life of herbs is limited. However, it can be prolonged with suitable storage. The place should be dark, rather cool and absolutely dry. A wooden medicine cabinet, placed not directly next to a source of heat, would be ideal. Never buy large quantities of herbs so as not to have to throw them away. Label the container with the name of the herb and the date of harvesting or processing.

13 Other dietic-books

The following syndromes of dietetics, TCM or for a therapy supplement for cancer are available.

Dietetics

E001. Nutrition of the infant - baby food
E002. Nutrition during lactation
E003. Nutrition in old age
E004. Nutrition of children and adolescents
E005. Nutrition of athletes
E006. Light weight
E007. Pregnancy
E008. Full food

Protein and electrolyte - kidneys
E009. (hemodialysis) dialysis treatment
E010. Acute renal failure
E011. Chronic renal insufficiency
E012. Nephrotic syndrome
E013. Kidney stones (nephrolithiasis)

Gastrointestinal tract - pancreas
E014. Acute pancreatitis (inflammation of the pancreas)
E015. Chronic pancreatitis (inflammation of the pancreas)

Gastrointestinal tract - small intestine and large intestine
E016. Acute obstipation (constipation)
E017. Chronic obstipation (constipation)
E018. Colon irritabile
E019. Diverticulitis
E020. Acquired lactose intolerance (lactose malabsorption)
E021. Fructose malabsorption
E022. Glutensensitive enteropathy (celiac disease)
E023. Colectomy
E024. Short Bowel Syndrome

Gastrointestinal tract - liver, gallbladder, bile ducts
E025. Acute and chronic hepatitis (inflammation of the liver)
E026. Cholelithiasis (bile stones)
E027. fatty liver
E028. cirrhosis

Gastrointestinal tract - Stomach and duodenal intestine
E029. Acute gastritis
E030. Chronic gastritis
E031. Stomach bleeding
E032. Ulcus ventriculi and duodenal ulcer
E033. Condition after gastric surgery

Gastrointestinal tract - oral cavity and esophagus
E034. Stomatitis
E035. Esophageal carcinoma (esophageal cancer)
E036. Refluosophagitis (heartburn)

Special diseases
E037. Phenylketonuria (PKU)
E038. Rheumatic joint diseases

Metabolism
E039. Obesity (overweight)
E040. Diabetes mellitus
E041. Eating disorders (underweight)

Fat metabolism
E042. Hypercholesterolaemia (increased cholesterol level)
E043. Hepatic Encephalopathy

Heart and circulation
E044. Arteriosclerosis (arterial calcification)
E045. Heart insufficiency
E046. Hypertension
E047. Hyperuricaemia and gout

Changed nutrient requirements
E048. In case of fever
E049. For malignant diseases
E050. After burns
E051. Radiation and chemotherapy

CANCER
E100. Pancreatic cancer
E101. Bladder cancer
E102. Blood cancer (leukemia)
E103. Breast cancer
E104. Colorectal cancer
E105. Gastric cancer
E106. Kidney cancer
E107. Esophageal cancer

TCM
E200. Bladder - moisture heat in the bladder
E201. Bladder - moisture and cold in the bladder
E202. Bladder - emptiness and cold in the bladder
E203. Large intestine - external cold affects the large intestine
E204. Large intestine - moisture heat in the large intestine
E205. Large intestine - heat blocks the intestine II acute
E206. Large intestine - dryness of the colon
E207. Large intestine - Yang deficiency (cold)
E208. Heart - Blood insufficiency
E209. Heart - Blood stagnation
E210. Heart - Fire
E211. Heart - Hot mucus clogs the heart pores

E212. Heart - Cold mucus clogs the heart pores
E213. Heart - Qi deficiency
E214. Heart - Yang deficiency
E215. Heart - Yin deficiency
E216. Liver - Ascending Liver Yang
E217. Liver - Blood deficiency
E218. Liver - Blood stagnation
E219. Liver - Moisture heat in liver and gall bladder
E220. Liver - Fire
E221. Liver - Gall bladder Qi-Empty
E222. Liver - Cold in the liver meridian
E223. Liver - Qi stagnation
E224. Liver - Wind
E225. Liver - Wind with ascending liver Yang
E226. Liver - Wind with blood anemic
E227. Liver - Wind with extreme heat
E228. Lung - Qi deficiency
E229. Lung - Mucus-moisture in the lungs
E230. Lung - Mucus-heat in the lungs
E231. Lung - Mucus-cold in the lungs
E232. Lung - Dryness of the lungs
E233. Lung - Wind-heat attacks the lungs
E234. Lung - Wind-cold affects the lungs
E235. Lung - Yin deficiency
E236. Stomach - Bloodstagnation
E237. Stomach - Fire
E238. Stomach - Cold with liquid
E239. Stomach - Nutrition stagnation
E240. Stomach - Qi deficiency
E241. Stomach - Rebelllous Qi
E242. Stomach - Yin Emptiness
E243. Spleen - Heat and moisture attack the spleen
E244. Spleen - Coldness and moisture affects the spleen
E245. Spleen - Qi deficiency
E246. Spleen - Qi deficiency + Declining spleen Qi
E247. Spleen - Qi deficiency + spleen does not control the blood
E248. Spleen - Yang deficiency
E249. Kidney - Heart and kidney no longer communicate
E250. Kidney - Jing deficiency
E251. Kidney - Kidneys cannot receive the Qi
E252. Kidney - Qi is not stable
E253. Kidney - Yang deficiency
E254. Kidney - Yin deficiency

For further information visit di-book.com.

14 EBNS - Software for nutritional counseling

The main task of the database is to create personalized nutritional advice for each patient individually. The database was developed for Dietetics and Traditional Chinese Medicine.
The Database supports training and advices in the daily work routine.

The computer program provides lists of recipes, ingredients and herbs, which are given to the client. individually adjustable according to patient's request from whole food to vegetarians (lacto, ovo, ...). For every register there is an information sheet which can be given to the client. All texts can be individually designed.

The syndromes can be combined and result in an intersection of the recommended recipes and ingredients. The automated diagnosis for the TCM enables you to check your experience during the training as well as to confirm your diagnosis in the working day. You select several predefined symptoms and have the program automatically display the relevant syndromes.

How to work with the database:
Select the patient / client, select one or more of the syndromes you diagnosed and print the folder.

You can change all values, create new symptoms or syndromes, develop recipes, change or adapt ingredients and herbs to your findings. In simple client management, all relevant data about the person is stored. You get an overview of the past diagnoses and the development of the course of the disease.

As a consultant you save a lot of time when you print out the recipe, food and herbal lists for the recognized syndromes and give them to the clients. You can use this time for a personal conversation. With the database, dieticians and nutritionists can view the nutrients and trace elements for each recipe and develop recipes for syndromes even with suggested ingredients.

All recipe and grocery lists can also be ordered from me as a combination of several diseases. I wish all readers good luck, health and happiness in life.
More information can be found at www.ebns.at.
Volunteer: www.krebsinfo.at
Josef Miligui